Coding Interview

Contents

1	Rotate Array in Java	9
2	Evaluate Reverse Polish Notation	11
3	Isomorphic Strings	14
4	Word Ladder	15
5	Median of Two Sorted Arrays Java	18
6	Regular Expression Matching in Java	20
7	Merge Intervals	22
8	Insert Interval	24
9	Two Sum	26
10	Two Sum II Input array is sorted	27
11	Two Sum III Data structure design	28
12	3Sum	29
13	4Sum	31
14	3Sum Closest	33
15	String to Integer (atoi)	34
16	Merge Sorted Array	35
17	Valid Parentheses	36
18	Implement strStr()	37
19	Minimum Size Subarray Sum	39
20	Search Insert Position	41

Contents

21	Longest Consecutive Sequence	42
22	Valid Palindrome	44
23	ZigZag Conversion	47
24	Add Binary	48
25	Length of Last Word	49
26	Triangle	50
27	Contains Duplicate	52
28	Contains Duplicate II	52
29	Remove Duplicates from Sorted Array	53
30	Remove Duplicates from Sorted Array II	55
31	Longest Substring Without Repeating Characters	58
32	Longest Substring Which Contains 2 Unique Characters	60
33	Minimum Window Substring	63
34	Reverse Words in a String	64
35	Find Minimum in Rotated Sorted Array	65
36	Find Minimum in Rotated Sorted Array II	66
37	Find Peak Element	68
38	Min Stack	68
39	Majority Element	70
40	Remove Element	71
41	Largest Rectangle in Histogram	71
42	Longest Common Prefix	73
43	Largest Number	74
44	Simplify Path	75
45	Compare Version Numbers	76

Contents

46	Gas Station	77
47	Pascal's Triangle	79
48	Pascal's Triangle II	80
49	Container With Most Water	81
50	Count and Say	82
51	Search for a Range	83
52	Kth Largest Element in an Array	84
53	Anagrams	86
54	First Missing Positive	87
55	Shortest Palindrome	88
56	Set Matrix Zeroes	89
57	Spiral Matrix	91
58	Spiral Matrix II	94
59	Search a 2D Matrix	95
60	Rotate Image	96
61	Valid Sudoku	98
62	Minimum Path Sum	99
63	Unique Paths	101
64	Unique Paths II	102
65	Number of Islands	104
66	Surrounded Regions	105
67	Maximal Rectangle	109
68	Add Two Numbers	110
69	Reorder List	114
70	Linked List Cycle	118

71	Copy List with Random Pointer	119
72	Merge Two Sorted Lists	121
73	Merge k Sorted Lists	123
74	Remove Duplicates from Sorted List	124
75	Partition List	126
76	LRU Cache	128
77	Intersection of Two Linked Lists	131
78	Remove Linked List Elements	132
79	Swap Nodes in Pairs	133
80	Reverse Linked List	134
81	Remove Nth Node From End of List	135
82	Java PriorityQueue Class Example	137
83	Solution for Binary Tree Preorder Traversal in Java	139
84	Solution of Binary Tree Inorder Traversal in Java	140
85	Solution of Iterative Binary Tree Postorder Traversal in Java	141
86	Binary Tree Level Order Traversal	143
87	Binary Tree Level Order Traversal II	144
88	Validate Binary Search Tree	145
89	Flatten Binary Tree to Linked List	147
90	Path Sum	148
91	Path Sum II	150
92	Construct Binary Tree from Inorder and Postorder Traversal	151
93	Convert Sorted Array to Binary Search Tree	153
94	Convert Sorted List to Binary Search Tree	154
95	Minimum Depth of Binary Tree	156

Contents

96	Binary Tree Maximum Path Sum	157
97	Balanced Binary Tree	158
98	Symmetric Tree	159
99	Binary Search Tree Iterator	160
100	Binary Tree Right Side View	162
101	Implement Trie (Prefix Tree)	163
102	Add and Search Word Data structure design	165
103	Merge K Sorted Arrays in Java	168
104	Populating Next Right Pointers in Each Node	169
105	Unique Binary Search Trees	171
106	Unique Binary Search Trees II	173
107	Sum Root to Leaf Numbers	174
108	Clone Graph Java	176
109	Course Schedule	178
110	How Developers Sort in Java?	181
111	Solution Merge Sort LinkedList in Java	182
112	Quicksort Array in Java	186
113	Solution Sort a linked list using insertion sort in Java	187
114	Maximum Gap	190
115	Edit Distance in Java	191
116	Longest Palindromic Substring	194
117	Word Break	198
118	Word Break II	200
119	Maximum Subarray	203
120	Maximum Product Subarray	204

121 Palindrome Partitioning	206
122 Palindrome Partitioning II	208
123 Candy	209
124 Jump Game	210
125 Best Time to Buy and Sell Stock	211
126 Best Time to Buy and Sell Stock II	212
127 Best Time to Buy and Sell Stock III	213
128 Best Time to Buy and Sell Stock IV	214
129 Dungeon Game	216
130 House Robber	217
131 House Robber II	218
132 Distinct Subsequences Total	220
133 Single Number	222
134 Single Number II	222
135 Twitter Codility Problem Max Binary Gap	223
136 Number of 1 Bits	224
137 Reverse Bits	224
138 Repeated DNA Sequences	225
139 Bitwise AND of Numbers Range	227
140 Permutations	227
141 Permutations II	229
142 Permutation Sequence	231
143 Generate Parentheses	233
144 Combination Sum	235
145 Combination Sum II	236

Contents

146 Combination Sum III 237

147 Combinations 238

148 Letter Combinations of a Phone Number 240

149 Reverse Integer 242

150 Palindrome Number 243

151 Pow(x, n) 244

1 Rotate Array in Java

You may have been using Java for a while. Do you think a simple Java array question can be a challenge? Let's use the following problem to test.

Problem: Rotate an array of n elements to the right by k steps. For example, with n = 7 and k = 3, the array [1,2,3,4,5,6,7] is rotated to [5,6,7,1,2,3,4]. How many different ways do you know to solve this problem?

1.1 Solution 1 - Intermediate Array

In a straightforward way, we can create a new array and then copy elements to the new array. Then change the original array by using System.arraycopy().

```java
public void rotate(int[] nums, int k) {
   if(k > nums.length)
      k=k%nums.length;

   int[] result = new int[nums.length];

   for(int i=0; i < k; i++){
      result[i] = nums[nums.length-k+i];
   }

   int j=0;
   for(int i=k; i<nums.length; i++){
      result[i] = nums[j];
      j++;
   }

   System.arraycopy( result, 0, nums, 0, nums.length );
}
```

Space is O(n) and time is O(n). You can check out the difference between System.arraycopy() and Arrays.copyOf().

1.2 Solution 2 - Bubble Rotate

Can we do this in O(1) space?
This solution is like a bubble sort.

```java
public static void rotate(int[] arr, int order) {
   if (arr == null || order < 0) {
```

1 Rotate Array in Java

```java
        throw new IllegalArgumentException("Illegal argument!");
    }

    for (int i = 0; i < order; i++) {
        for (int j = arr.length - 1; j > 0; j--) {
            int temp = arr[j];
            arr[j] = arr[j - 1];
            arr[j - 1] = temp;
        }
    }
}
```

However, the time is O(n*k).

Here is an example (length=7, order=3):

```
i=0
0 1 2 3 4 5 6
0 1 2 3 4 6 5
...
6 0 1 2 3 4 5
i=1
6 0 1 2 3 5 4
...
5 6 0 1 2 3 4
i=2
5 6 0 1 2 4 3
...
4 5 6 0 1 2 3
```

1.3 Solution 3 - Reversal

Can we do this in O(1) space and in O(n) time? The following solution does.

Assuming we are given 1,2,3,4,5,6 and order 2. The basic idea is:

```
1. Divide the array two parts: 1,2,3,4 and 5, 6
2. Rotate first part: 4,3,2,1,5,6
3. Rotate second part: 4,3,2,1,6,5
4. Rotate the whole array: 5,6,1,2,3,4
```

```java
public static void rotate(int[] arr, int order) {
    order = order % arr.length;

    if (arr == null || order < 0) {
        throw new IllegalArgumentException("Illegal argument!");
    }

    //length of first part
    int a = arr.length - order;
```

```
    reverse(arr, 0, a-1);
    reverse(arr, a, arr.length-1);
    reverse(arr, 0, arr.length-1);

}

public static void reverse(int[] arr, int left, int right){
    if(arr == null || arr.length == 1)
        return;

    while(left < right){
        int temp = arr[left];
        arr[left] = arr[right];
        arr[right] = temp;
        left++;
        right--;
    }
}
```

2 Evaluate Reverse Polish Notation

Evaluate the value of an arithmetic expression in Reverse Polish Notation. Valid operators are +, -, *, /. Each operand may be an integer or another expression. For example:

```
["2", "1", "+", "3", "*"] -> ((2 + 1) * 3) -> 9
["4", "13", "5", "/", "+"] -> (4 + (13 / 5)) -> 6
```

2.1 Naive Approach

This problem can be solved by using a stack. We can loop through each element in the given array. When it is a number, push it to the stack. When it is an operator, pop two numbers from the stack, do the calculation, and push back the result.

2 Evaluate Reverse Polish Notation

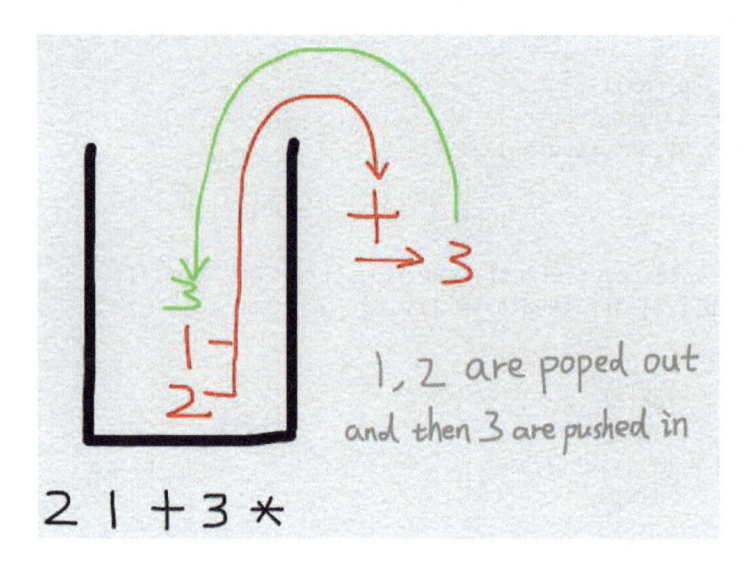

The following is the code. However, this code contains compilation errors in leetcode. Why?

```java
public class Test {

  public static void main(String[] args) throws IOException {
    String[] tokens = new String[] { "2", "1", "+", "3", "*" };
    System.out.println(evalRPN(tokens));
  }

  public static int evalRPN(String[] tokens) {
    int returnValue = 0;
    String operators = "+-*/";

    Stack<String> stack = new Stack<String>();

    for (String t : tokens) {
      if (!operators.contains(t)) { //push to stack if it is a number
        stack.push(t);
      } else {//pop numbers from stack if it is an operator
        int a = Integer.valueOf(stack.pop());
        int b = Integer.valueOf(stack.pop());
        switch (t) {
        case "+":
          stack.push(String.valueOf(a + b));
          break;
        case "-":
          stack.push(String.valueOf(b - a));
          break;
        case "*":
          stack.push(String.valueOf(a * b));
          break;
```

2 Evaluate Reverse Polish Notation

```
        case "/":
          stack.push(String.valueOf(b / a));
          break;
        }
      }
    }

    returnValue = Integer.valueOf(stack.pop());

    return returnValue;
  }
}
```

The problem is that switch string statement is only available from JDK 1.7. Leetcode apparently use a JDK version below 1.7.

2.2 Accepted Solution

If you want to use switch statement, you can convert the above by using the following code which use the index of a string "+-*/".

```
public class Solution {
  public int evalRPN(String[] tokens) {

    int returnValue = 0;

    String operators = "+-*/";

    Stack<String> stack = new Stack<String>();

    for(String t : tokens){
      if(!operators.contains(t)){
        stack.push(t);
      }else{
        int a = Integer.valueOf(stack.pop());
        int b = Integer.valueOf(stack.pop());
        int index = operators.indexOf(t);
        switch(index){
          case 0:
            stack.push(String.valueOf(a+b));
            break;
          case 1:
            stack.push(String.valueOf(b-a));
            break;
          case 2:
            stack.push(String.valueOf(a*b));
            break;
          case 3:
            stack.push(String.valueOf(b/a));
```

```
            break;
        }
    }
}

    returnValue = Integer.valueOf(stack.pop());

    return returnValue;

    }
}
```

3 Isomorphic Strings

Given two strings s and t, determine if they are isomorphic. Two strings are isomorphic if the characters in s can be replaced to get t.

For example,"egg" and "add" are isomorphic, "foo" and "bar" are not.

3.1 Analysis

We need to define a method which accepts a map & a value, and returns the value's key in the map.

3.2 Java Solution

```java
public boolean isIsomorphic(String s, String t) {
    if(s==null || t==null)
        return false;

    if(s.length() != t.length())
        return false;

    if(s.length()==0 && t.length()==0)
        return true;

    HashMap<Character, Character> map = new HashMap<Character,Character>();
    for(int i=0; i<s.length(); i++){
        char c1 = s.charAt(i);
        char c2 = t.charAt(i);

        Character c = getKey(map, c2);
        if(c != null && c!=c1){
            return false;
```

```
        }else if(map.containsKey(c1)){
            if(c2 != map.get(c1))
                return false;
        }else{
            map.put(c1,c2);
        }
    }

    return true;
}

// a method for getting key of a target value
public Character getKey(HashMap<Character,Character> map, Character target){
    for (Map.Entry<Character,Character> entry : map.entrySet()) {
        if (entry.getValue().equals(target)) {
            return entry.getKey();
        }
    }

    return null;
}
```

4 Word Ladder

Given two words (start and end), and a dictionary, find the length of shortest transformation sequence from start to end, such that only one letter can be changed at a time and each intermediate word must exist in the dictionary. For example, given:

```
start = "hit"
end = "cog"
dict = ["hot","dot","dog","lot","log"]
```

One shortest transformation is "hit" ->"hot" ->"dot" ->"dog" ->"cog", the program should return its length 5.

Note: Return 0 if there is no such transformation sequence. All words have the same length. All words contain only lowercase alphabetic characters.

4.1 Naive Approach

In a simplest way, we can start from start word, change one character each time, if it is in the dictionary, we continue with the replaced word, until start == end.

```
public class Solution {
    public int ladderLength(String start, String end, HashSet<String> dict) {
```

4 Word Ladder

```
        int len=0;
        HashSet<String> visited = new HashSet<String>();

        for(int i=0; i<start.length(); i++){
            char[] startArr = start.toCharArray();

            for(char c='a'; c<='z'; c++){
                if(c==start.toCharArray()[i]){
                    continue;
                }

                startArr[i] = c;
                String temp = new String(startArr);
                if(dict.contains(temp)){
                    len++;
                    start = temp;
                    if(temp.equals(end)){
                        return len;
                    }
                }
            }
        }

        return len;
    }
}
```

This solution is wrong. The following example shows the problem. It can not find the shortest path. The output is 3, but it actually only takes 2.

```
Input: "a", "c", ["a","b","c"]
Output: 3
Expected: 2
```

4.2 Breath First Search

So we quickly realize that this looks like a tree searching problem for which breath first guarantees the optimal solution.

Assuming we have some words in the dictionary, and the start is "hit" as shown in the diagram below.

4 Word Ladder

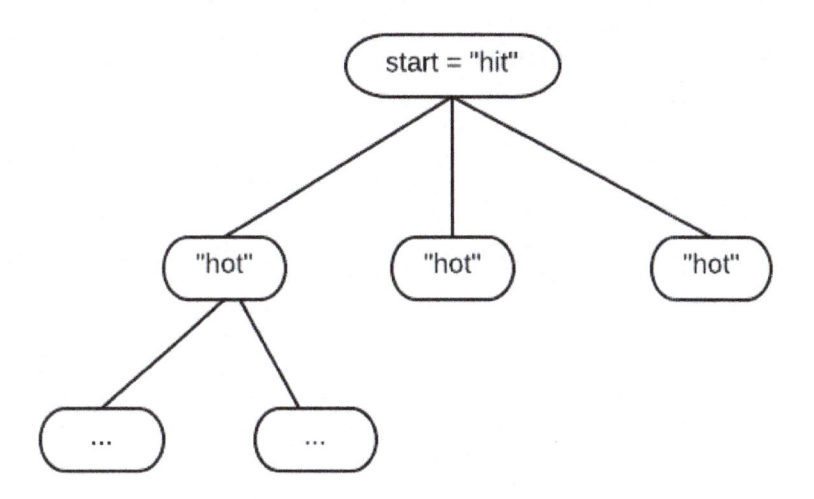

We can use two queues to traverse the tree, one stores the nodes, the other stores the step numbers.

```java
public int ladderLength(String start, String end, HashSet<String> dict) {
  if (dict.size() == 0)
    return 0;

  dict.add(end);

  LinkedList<String> wordQueue = new LinkedList<String>();
  LinkedList<Integer> distanceQueue = new LinkedList<Integer>();

  wordQueue.add(start);
  distanceQueue.add(1);

  //track the shortest path
  int result = Integer.MAX_VALUE;
  while (!wordQueue.isEmpty()) {
    String currWord = wordQueue.pop();
    Integer currDistance = distanceQueue.pop();

    if (currWord.equals(end)) {
      result = Math.min(result, currDistance);
    }

    for (int i = 0; i < currWord.length(); i++) {
      char[] currCharArr = currWord.toCharArray();
      for (char c = 'a'; c <= 'z'; c++) {
        currCharArr[i] = c;

        String newWord = new String(currCharArr);
        if (dict.contains(newWord)) {
```

```
            wordQueue.add(newWord);
            distanceQueue.add(currDistance + 1);
            dict.remove(newWord);
          }
        }
      }
    }

    if (result < Integer.MAX_VALUE)
      return result;
    else
      return 0;
}
```

4.3 What can be learned from this problem?

- Use breath-first or depth-first search to solve problems
- Use two queues, one for words and another for counting

5 Median of Two Sorted Arrays Java

There are two sorted arrays A and B of size m and n respectively. Find the median of the two sorted arrays. The overall run time complexity should be O(log (m+n)).

5.1 Analysis

If we see log(n), we should think about using binary something.
  This problem can be converted to the problem of finding kth element, k is (A's length + B' Length)/2.
  If any of the two arrays is empty, then the kth element is the non-empty array's kth element. If k == 0, the kth element is the first element of A or B.

5.2 For normal cases(all other cases), we need to move the pointer at the pace of half of an array length to get log(n) time. Java Solution

```java
public static double findMedianSortedArrays(int A[], int B[]) {
    int m = A.length;
```

```java
    int n = B.length;

    if ((m + n) % 2 != 0) // odd
      return (double) findKth(A, B, (m + n) / 2, 0, m - 1, 0, n - 1);
    else { // even
      return (findKth(A, B, (m + n) / 2, 0, m - 1, 0, n - 1)
        + findKth(A, B, (m + n) / 2 - 1, 0, m - 1, 0, n - 1)) * 0.5;
    }
}

public static int findKth(int A[], int B[], int k,
  int aStart, int aEnd, int bStart, int bEnd) {

  int aLen = aEnd - aStart + 1;
  int bLen = bEnd - bStart + 1;

  // Handle special cases
  if (aLen == 0)
    return B[bStart + k];
  if (bLen == 0)
    return A[aStart + k];
  if (k == 0)
    return A[aStart] < B[bStart] ? A[aStart] : B[bStart];

  int aMid = aLen * k / (aLen + bLen); // a's middle count
  int bMid = k - aMid - 1; // b's middle count

  // make aMid and bMid to be array index
  aMid = aMid + aStart;
  bMid = bMid + bStart;

  if (A[aMid] > B[bMid]) {
    k = k - (bMid - bStart + 1);
    aEnd = aMid;
    bStart = bMid + 1;
  } else {
    k = k - (aMid - aStart + 1);
    bEnd = bMid;
    aStart = aMid + 1;
  }

  return findKth(A, B, k, aStart, aEnd, bStart, bEnd);
}
```

5.3 The Steps of the Algorithm

Thanks to Gunner86. The description of the algorithm is awesome!

```
1) Calculate the medians m1 and m2 of the input arrays ar1[] and ar2[]
   respectively.
2) If m1 and m2 both are equal then we are done, and return m1 (or m2)
3) If m1 is greater than m2, then median is present in one of the below two
   subarrays.
a) From first element of ar1 to m1 (ar1[0...|_n/2_|])
b) From m2 to last element of ar2 (ar2[|_n/2_|...n-1])
4) If m2 is greater than m1, then median is present in one of the below two
   subarrays.
a) From m1 to last element of ar1 (ar1[|_n/2_|...n-1])
b) From first element of ar2 to m2 (ar2[0...|_n/2_|])
5) Repeat the above process until size of both the subarrays becomes 2.
6) If size of the two arrays is 2 then use below formula to get the median.
Median = (max(ar1[0], ar2[0]) + min(ar1[1], ar2[1]))/2
```

6 Regular Expression Matching in Java

Implement regular expression matching with support for '.' and '*'.

'.' Matches any single character. '*' Matches zero or more of the preceding element.

The matching should cover the entire input string (not partial).

The function prototype should be: bool isMatch(const char *s, const char *p)

Some examples: isMatch("aa","a") return false isMatch("aa","aa") return true isMatch("aaa","aa") return false isMatch("aa", "a*") return true isMatch("aa", ".*") return true isMatch("ab", ".*") return true isMatch("aab", "c*a*b") return true

6.1 Analysis

First of all, this is one of the most difficulty problems. It is hard to think through all different cases. The problem should be simplified to handle 2 basic cases:

- the second char of pattern is "*"
- the second char of pattern is not "*"

For the 1st case, if the first char of pattern is not ".", the first char of pattern and string should be the same. Then continue to match the remaining part.

For the 2nd case, if the first char of pattern is "." or first char of pattern == the first i char of string, continue to match the remaining part.

6.2 Java Solution 1 (Short)

The following Java solution is accepted

```java
public class Solution {
    public boolean isMatch(String s, String p) {

        if(p.length() == 0)
            return s.length() == 0;

        //p's length 1 is special case
        if(p.length() == 1 || p.charAt(1) != '*'){
            if(s.length() < 1 || (p.charAt(0) != '.' && s.charAt(0) !=
                p.charAt(0)))
                return false;
            return isMatch(s.substring(1), p.substring(1));

        }else{
            int len = s.length();

            int i = -1;
            while(i<len && (i < 0 || p.charAt(0) == '.' || p.charAt(0) ==
                s.charAt(i))){
                if(isMatch(s.substring(i+1), p.substring(2)))
                    return true;
                i++;
            }
            return false;
        }
    }
}
```

6.3 Java Solution 2 (More Readable)

```java
public boolean isMatch(String s, String p) {
  // base case
  if (p.length() == 0) {
    return s.length() == 0;
  }

  // special case
  if (p.length() == 1) {

    // if the length of s is 0, return false
    if (s.length() < 1) {
      return false;
    }

    //if the first does not match, return false
    else if ((p.charAt(0) != s.charAt(0)) && (p.charAt(0) != '.')) {
      return false;
```

```
      }

      // otherwise, compare the rest of the string of s and p.
      else {
        return isMatch(s.substring(1), p.substring(1));
      }
    }

    // case 1: when the second char of p is not '*'
    if (p.charAt(1) != '*') {
      if (s.length() < 1) {
        return false;
      }
      if ((p.charAt(0) != s.charAt(0)) && (p.charAt(0) != '.')) {
        return false;
      } else {
        return isMatch(s.substring(1), p.substring(1));
      }
    }

    // case 2: when the second char of p is '*', complex case.
    else {
      //case 2.1: a char & '*' can stand for 0 element
      if (isMatch(s, p.substring(2))) {
        return true;
      }

      //case 2.2: a char & '*' can stand for 1 or more preceding element,
      //so try every sub string
      int i = 0;
      while (i<s.length() && (s.charAt(i)==p.charAt(0) || p.charAt(0)=='.')){
        if (isMatch(s.substring(i + 1), p.substring(2))) {
          return true;
        }
        i++;
      }
      return false;
    }
  }
```

7 Merge Intervals

Problem:

Given a collection of intervals, merge all overlapping intervals.

For example,
Given [1,3],[2,6],[8,10],[15,18],
return [1,6],[8,10],[15,18].

7.1 Thoughts of This Problem

The key to solve this problem is defining a Comparator first to sort the arraylist of Intevals. And then merge some intervals.

The take-away message from this problem is utilizing the advantage of sorted list/array.

7.2 Java Solution

```java
class Interval {
  int start;
  int end;

  Interval() {
    start = 0;
    end = 0;
  }

  Interval(int s, int e) {
    start = s;
    end = e;
  }
}

public class Solution {
  public ArrayList<Interval> merge(ArrayList<Interval> intervals) {

    if (intervals == null || intervals.size() <= 1)
      return intervals;

    // sort intervals by using self-defined Comparator
    Collections.sort(intervals, new IntervalComparator());

    ArrayList<Interval> result = new ArrayList<Interval>();

    Interval prev = intervals.get(0);
    for (int i = 1; i < intervals.size(); i++) {
      Interval curr = intervals.get(i);

      if (prev.end >= curr.start) {
        // merged case
```

```java
            Interval merged = new Interval(prev.start, Math.max(prev.end,
                curr.end));
            prev = merged;
        } else {
            result.add(prev);
            prev = curr;
        }
    }

    result.add(prev);

    return result;
  }
}

class IntervalComparator implements Comparator<Interval> {
  public int compare(Interval i1, Interval i2) {
    return i1.start - i2.start;
  }
}
```

8 Insert Interval

Problem:

> Given a set of non-overlapping & sorted intervals, insert a new interval into the intervals (merge if necessary).

Example 1:
Given intervals [1,3],[6,9], insert and merge [2,5] in as [1,5],[6,9].

Example 2:
Given [1,2],[3,5],[6,7],[8,10],[12,16], insert and merge [4,9] in as
    [1,2],[3,10],[12,16].

This is because the new interval [4,9] overlaps with [3,5],[6,7],[8,10].

8.1 Thoughts of This Problem

Quickly summarize 3 cases. Whenever there is intersection, created a new interval.

8 Insert Interval

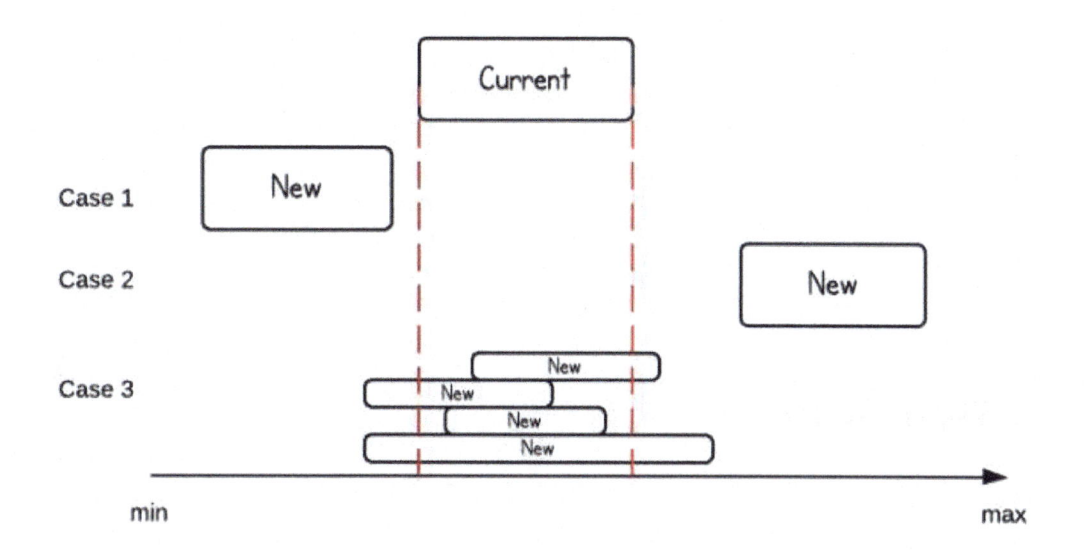

8.2 Java Solution

```java
/**
 * Definition for an interval.
 * public class Interval {
 *     int start;
 *     int end;
 *     Interval() { start = 0; end = 0; }
 *     Interval(int s, int e) { start = s; end = e; }
 * }
 */
public class Solution {
    public ArrayList<Interval> insert(ArrayList<Interval> intervals, Interval
        newInterval) {

        ArrayList<Interval> result = new ArrayList<Interval>();

        for(Interval interval: intervals){
            if(interval.end < newInterval.start){
                result.add(interval);
            }else if(interval.start > newInterval.end){
                result.add(newInterval);
                newInterval = interval;
            }else if(interval.end >= newInterval.start || interval.start <=
                newInterval.end){
                newInterval = new Interval(Math.min(interval.start,
                    newInterval.start), Math.max(newInterval.end, interval.end));
            }
        }
    }
```

```
        result.add(newInterval);

        return result;
    }
}
```

9 Two Sum

Given an array of integers, find two numbers such that they add up to a specific target number.

The function twoSum should return indices of the two numbers such that they add up to the target, where index1 must be less than index2. Please note that your returned answers (both index1 and index2) are not zero-based.

For example:

```
Input: numbers={2, 7, 11, 15}, target=9
Output: index1=1, index2=2
```

9.1 Naive Approach

This problem is pretty straightforward. We can simply examine every possible pair of numbers in this integer array.

Time complexity in worst case: $O(n^2)$.

```java
public static int[] twoSum(int[] numbers, int target) {
    int[] ret = new int[2];
    for (int i = 0; i < numbers.length; i++) {
        for (int j = i + 1; j < numbers.length; j++) {
            if (numbers[i] + numbers[j] == target) {
                ret[0] = i + 1;
                ret[1] = j + 1;
            }
        }
    }
    return ret;
}
```

Can we do better?

9.2 Better Solution

Use HashMap to store the target value.

```java
public class Solution {
    public int[] twoSum(int[] numbers, int target) {
   HashMap<Integer, Integer> map = new HashMap<Integer, Integer>();
   int[] result = new int[2];

   for (int i = 0; i < numbers.length; i++) {
     if (map.containsKey(numbers[i])) {
       int index = map.get(numbers[i]);
       result[0] = index+1 ;
       result[1] = i+1;
       break;
     } else {
       map.put(target - numbers[i], i);
     }
   }

   return result;
    }
}
```

Time complexity depends on the put and get operations of HashMap which is normally O(1).

Time complexity of this solution is O(n).

10 Two Sum II

Input array is sorted

This problem is similar to Two Sum.

To solve this problem, we can use two points to scan the array from both sides. See Java solution below:

```java
public int[] twoSum(int[] numbers, int target) {
  if (numbers == null || numbers.length == 0)
    return null;

  int i = 0;
  int j = numbers.length - 1;

  while (i < j) {
    int x = numbers[i] + numbers[j];
    if (x < target) {
      ++i;
```

```
    } else if (x > target) {
      j--;
    } else {
      return new int[] { i + 1, j + 1 };
    }
  }

  return null;
}
```

11 Two Sum III Data structure design

Design and implement a TwoSum class. It should support the following operations: add and find.

add - Add the number to an internal data structure. find - Find if there exists any pair of numbers which sum is equal to the value.

For example,

```
add(1);
add(3);
add(5);
find(4) -> true
find(7) -> false
```

11.1 Java Solution

Since the desired class need add and get operations, HashMap is a good option for this purpose.

```java
public class TwoSum {
  private HashMap<Integer, Integer> elements = new HashMap<Integer,
      Integer>();

  public void add(int number) {
    if (elements.containsKey(number)) {
      elements.put(number, elements.get(number) + 1);
    } else {
      elements.put(number, 1);
    }
  }

  public boolean find(int value) {
    for (Integer i : elements.keySet()) {
      int target = value - i;
```

```
            if (elements.containsKey(target)) {
               if (i == target && elements.get(target) < 2) {
                  continue;
               }
               return true;
            }
         }
      }
      return false;
   }
}
```

12 3Sum

Problem:

Given an array S of n integers, are there elements a, b, c in S such that a + b + c = 0?
Find all unique triplets in the array which gives the sum of zero.

Note: Elements in a triplet (a,b,c) must be in non-descending order. (ie, $a \leq b \leq c$)
The solution set must not contain duplicate triplets.

```
For example, given array S = {-1 0 1 2 -1 -4},

   A solution set is:
   (-1, 0, 1)
   (-1, -1, 2)
```

12.1 Naive Solution

Naive solution is 3 loops, and this gives time complexity $O(n^3)$. Apparently this is not an acceptable solution, but a discussion can start from here.

```java
public class Solution {
   public ArrayList<ArrayList<Integer>> threeSum(int[] num) {
      //sort array
      Arrays.sort(num);

      ArrayList<ArrayList<Integer>> result = new
         ArrayList<ArrayList<Integer>>();
      ArrayList<Integer> each = new ArrayList<Integer>();
      for(int i=0; i<num.length; i++){
         if(num[i] > 0) break;

         for(int j=i+1; j<num.length; j++){
```

12 3Sum

```
            if(num[i] + num[j] > 0 && num[j] > 0) break;

            for(int k=j+1; k<num.length; k++){
              if(num[i] + num[j] + num[k] == 0) {

                 each.add(num[i]);
                 each.add(num[j]);
                 each.add(num[k]);
                 result.add(each);
                 each.clear();
              }
            }
          }
       }

       return result;
    }
}
```

* The solution also does not handle duplicates. Therefore, it is not only time inefficient, but also incorrect.
Result:

```
Submission Result: Output Limit Exceeded
```

12.2 Better Solution

A better solution is using two pointers instead of one. This makes time complexity of $O(n^2)$.

To avoid duplicate, we can take advantage of sorted arrays, i.e., move pointers by >1 to use same element only once.

```java
public ArrayList<ArrayList<Integer>> threeSum(int[] num) {
  ArrayList<ArrayList<Integer>> result = new ArrayList<ArrayList<Integer>>();

  if (num.length < 3)
    return result;

  // sort array
  Arrays.sort(num);

  for (int i = 0; i < num.length - 2; i++) {
    // //avoid duplicate solutions
    if (i == 0 || num[i] > num[i - 1]) {

      int negate = -num[i];

      int start = i + 1;
```

```java
        int end = num.length - 1;

        while (start < end) {
          //case 1
          if (num[start] + num[end] == negate) {
            ArrayList<Integer> temp = new ArrayList<Integer>();
            temp.add(num[i]);
            temp.add(num[start]);
            temp.add(num[end]);

            result.add(temp);
            start++;
            end--;
            //avoid duplicate solutions
            while (start < end && num[end] == num[end + 1])
              end--;

            while (start < end && num[start] == num[start - 1])
              start++;
          //case 2
          } else if (num[start] + num[end] < negate) {
            start++;
          //case 3
          } else {
            end--;
          }
        }

      }
    }

    return result;
}
```

13 4Sum

Given an array S of n integers, are there elements a, b, c, and d in S such that a + b + c + d = target? Find all unique quadruplets in the array which gives the sum of target.

Note: Elements in a quadruplet (a,b,c,d) must be in non-descending order. (ie, a $\leq$ b $\leq$ c $\leq$ d) The solution set must not contain duplicate quadruplets.

```
For example, given array S = {1 0 -1 0 -2 2}, and target = 0.

    A solution set is:
```

13 4Sum

```
(-1, 0, 0, 1)
(-2, -1, 1, 2)
(-2, 0, 0, 2)
```

13.1 Thoughts

A typical k-sum problem. Time is N to the power of (k-1).

13.2 Java Solution

```java
public ArrayList<ArrayList<Integer>> fourSum(int[] num, int target) {
  Arrays.sort(num);

  HashSet<ArrayList<Integer>> hashSet = new HashSet<ArrayList<Integer>>();
  ArrayList<ArrayList<Integer>> result = new ArrayList<ArrayList<Integer>>();

  for (int i = 0; i < num.length; i++) {
    for (int j = i + 1; j < num.length; j++) {
      int k = j + 1;
      int l = num.length - 1;

      while (k < l) {
        int sum = num[i] + num[j] + num[k] + num[l];

        if (sum > target) {
          l--;
        } else if (sum < target) {
          k++;
        } else if (sum == target) {
          ArrayList<Integer> temp = new ArrayList<Integer>();
          temp.add(num[i]);
          temp.add(num[j]);
          temp.add(num[k]);
          temp.add(num[l]);

          if (!hashSet.contains(temp)) {
            hashSet.add(temp);
            result.add(temp);
          }

          k++;
          l--;
        }
      }
    }
  }

  return result;
```

}

Here is the hashCode method of ArrayList. It makes sure that if all elements of two lists are the same, then the hash code of the two lists will be the same. Since each element in the ArrayList is Integer, same integer has same hash code.

```java
int hashCode = 1;
Iterator<E> i = list.iterator();
while (i.hasNext()) {
    E obj = i.next();
    hashCode = 31*hashCode + (obj==null ? 0 : obj.hashCode());
}
```

14 3Sum Closest

Given an array S of n integers, find three integers in S such that the sum is closest to a given number, target. Return the sum of the three integers. You may assume that each input would have exactly one solution. For example, given array S = -1 2 1 -4, and target = 1. The sum that is closest to the target is 2. (-1 + 2 + 1 = 2).

14.1 Thoughts

This problem is similar with 2 Sum. This kind of problem can be solve by using similar approach, i.e., two pointers from both left and right.

14.2 Java Solution

```java
public class Solution {
  public int threeSumClosest(int[] num, int target) {
    int min = Integer.MAX_VALUE;
    int result = 0;

    Arrays.sort(num);

    for (int i = 0; i < num.length; i++) {
      int j = i + 1;
      int k = num.length - 1;
      while (j < k) {
        int sum = num[i] + num[j] + num[k];
        int diff = Math.abs(sum - target);

        if(diff == 0) return 0;
```

```java
            if (diff < min) {
               min = diff;
               result = sum;
            }
            if (sum <= target) {
               j++;
            } else {
               k--;
            }
         }
      }
   }

   return result;
}
```

Time Complexity is O(n²).

15 String to Integer (atoi)

Implement atoi to convert a string to an integer.

Hint: Carefully consider all possible input cases. If you want a challenge, please do not see below and ask yourself what are the possible input cases.

15.1 Analysis

The following cases should be considered for this problem:

1. `null` or empty string
2. white spaces
3. +/- sign
4. calculate real value
5. handle min & max

15.2 Java Solution

```java
public int atoi(String str) {
   if (str == null || str.length() < 1)
      return 0;

   // trim white spaces
```

```java
    str = str.trim();

    char flag = '+';

    // check negative or positive
    int i = 0;
    if (str.charAt(0) == '-') {
        flag = '-';
        i++;
    } else if (str.charAt(0) == '+') {
        i++;
    }
    // use double to store result
    double result = 0;

    // calculate value
    while (str.length() > i && str.charAt(i) >= '0' && str.charAt(i) <= '9') {
        result = result * 10 + (str.charAt(i) - '0');
        i++;
    }

    if (flag == '-')
        result = -result;

    // handle max and min
    if (result > Integer.MAX_VALUE)
        return Integer.MAX_VALUE;

    if (result < Integer.MIN_VALUE)
        return Integer.MIN_VALUE;

    return (int) result;
}
```

16 Merge Sorted Array

Given two sorted integer arrays A and B, merge B into A as one sorted array.

Note: You may assume that A has enough space to hold additional elements from B. The number of elements initialized in A and B are m and n respectively.

16.1 Analysis

The key to solve this problem is moving element of A and B backwards. If B has some elements left after A is done, also need to handle that case.

The takeaway message from this problem is that the loop condition. This kind of condition is also used for merging two sorted linked list.

16.2 Java Solution 1

```java
public class Solution {
    public void merge(int A[], int m, int B[], int n) {

        while(m > 0 && n > 0){
            if(A[m-1] > B[n-1]){
                A[m+n-1] = A[m-1];
                m--;
            }else{
                A[m+n-1] = B[n-1];
                n--;
            }
        }

        while(n > 0){
            A[m+n-1] = B[n-1];
            n--;
        }
    }
}
```

16.3 Java Solution 2

The loop condition also can use m+n like the following.

```java
public void merge(int A[], int m, int B[], int n) {
  int i = m - 1;
  int j = n - 1;
  int k = m + n - 1;

  while (k >= 0) {
    if (j < 0 || (i >= 0 && A[i] > B[j]))
      A[k--] = A[i--];
    else
      A[k--] = B[j--];
  }
}
```

17 Valid Parentheses

Given a string containing just the characters '(', ')', '', '', '[' and ']', determine if the input string is valid. The brackets must close in the correct order, "()" and "()[]" are all valid but "(]" and "([)]" are not.

17.1 Analysis

17.2 Java Solution

```java
public static boolean isValid(String s) {
  HashMap<Character, Character> map = new HashMap<Character, Character>();
  map.put('(', ')');
  map.put('[', ']');
  map.put('{', '}');

  Stack<Character> stack = new Stack<Character>();

  for (int i = 0; i < s.length(); i++) {
    char curr = s.charAt(i);

    if (map.keySet().contains(curr)) {
      stack.push(curr);
    } else if (map.values().contains(curr)) {
      if (!stack.empty() && map.get(stack.peek()) == curr) {
        stack.pop();
      } else {
        return false;
      }
    }
  }

  return stack.empty();
}
```

18 Implement strStr()

Problem:

Implement strStr(). Returns the index of the first occurrence of needle in haystack, or -1 if needle is not part of haystack.

18.1 Java Solution 1 - Naive

```java
public int strStr(String haystack, String needle) {
    if(haystack==null || needle==null)
        return 0;

    if(needle.length() == 0)
        return 0;

    for(int i=0; i<haystack.length(); i++){
        if(i + needle.length() > haystack.length())
            return -1;

        int m = i;
        for(int j=0; j<needle.length(); j++){
            if(needle.charAt(j)==haystack.charAt(m)){
                if(j==needle.length()-1)
                    return i;
                m++;
            }else{
                break;
            }

        }
    }

    return -1;
}
```

18.2 Java Solution 2 - KMP

Check out this article to understand KMP algorithm.

```java
public int strStr(String haystack, String needle) {
    if(haystack==null || needle==null)
        return 0;

    int h = haystack.length();
    int n = needle.length();
```

```java
    if (n > h)
        return -1;
    if (n == 0)
        return 0;

    int[] next = getNext(needle);
    int i = 0;

    while (i <= h - n) {
        int success = 1;
        for (int j = 0; j < n; j++) {
            if (needle.charAt(0) != haystack.charAt(i)) {
                success = 0;
                i++;
                break;
            } else if (needle.charAt(j) != haystack.charAt(i + j)) {
                success = 0;
                i = i + j - next[j - 1];
                break;
            }
        }
        if (success == 1)
            return i;
    }

    return -1;
}

//calculate KMP array
public int[] getNext(String needle) {
    int[] next = new int[needle.length()];
    next[0] = 0;

    for (int i = 1; i < needle.length(); i++) {
        int index = next[i - 1];
        while (index > 0 && needle.charAt(index) != needle.charAt(i)) {
            index = next[index - 1];
        }

        if (needle.charAt(index) == needle.charAt(i)) {
            next[i] = next[i - 1] + 1;
        } else {
            next[i] = 0;
        }
    }

    return next;
}
```

19 Minimum Size Subarray Sum

Given an array of n positive integers and a positive integer s, find the minimal length of a subarray of which the sum ≥ s. If there isn't one, return 0 instead.

For example, given the array [2,3,1,2,4,3] and s = 7, the subarray [4,3] has the minimal length of 2 under the problem constraint.

19.1 Analysis

We can use 2 points to mark the left and right boundaries of the sliding window. When the sum is greater than the target, shift the left pointer; when the sum is less than the target, shift the right pointer.

19.2 Java Solution

```java
public int minSubArrayLen(int s, int[] nums) {
    if(nums == null || nums.length == 0){
        return 0;
    }

    // initialize min length to be the input array length
    int result = nums.length;

    int i = 0;
    int sum = nums[0];

    for(int j=0; j<nums.length; ){
        if(i==j){
            if(nums[i]>=s){
                return 1; //if single elem is large enough
            }else{
                j++;

                if(j<nums.length){
                    sum = sum + nums[j];
                }else{
                    return result;
                }
            }
        }else{
            //if sum is large enough, move left cursor
            if(sum >= s){
                result = Math.min(j-i+1, result);
```

```
            sum = sum - nums[i];
            i++;
        //if sum is not large enough, move right cursor
        }else{
            j++;

            if(j<nums.length){
                sum = sum + nums[j];
            }else{
                if(i==0){
                    return 0;
                }else{
                    return result;
                }
            }
        }
    }
}

    return result;
}
```

20 Search Insert Position

Given a sorted array and a target value, return the index if the target is found. If not, return the index where it would be if it were inserted in order. You may assume no duplicates in the array.

Here are few examples.

```
[1,3,5,6], 5 -> 2
[1,3,5,6], 2 -> 1
[1,3,5,6], 7 -> 4
[1,3,5,6], 0 -> 0
```

20.1 Solution 1

Naively, we can just iterate the array and compare target with ith and (i+1)th element. Time complexity is O(n)

```java
public class Solution {
    public int searchInsert(int[] A, int target) {

        if(A==null) return 0;
```

```
        if(target <= A[0]) return 0;

        for(int i=0; i<A.length-1; i++){
            if(target > A[i] && target <= A[i+1]){
                return i+1;
            }
        }

        return A.length;
    }
}
```

20.2 Solution 2

This also looks like a binary search problem. We should try to make the complexity to be O(log(n)).

```
public class Solution {
    public int searchInsert(int[] A, int target) {
        if(A==null||A.length==0)
            return 0;

        return searchInsert(A,target,0,A.length-1);
    }

    public int searchInsert(int[] A, int target, int start, int end){
        int mid=(start+end)/2;

        if(target==A[mid])
            return mid;
        else if(target<A[mid])
            return start<mid?searchInsert(A,target,start,mid-1):start;
        else
            return end>mid?searchInsert(A,target,mid+1,end):(end+1);
    }
}
```

21 Longest Consecutive Sequence

Given an unsorted array of integers, find the length of the longest consecutive elements sequence.

21 Longest Consecutive Sequence

For example, given [100, 4, 200, 1, 3, 2], the longest consecutive elements sequence should be [1, 2, 3, 4]. Its length is 4.

Your algorithm should run in O(n) complexity.

21.1 Analysis

Because it requires O(n) complexity, we can not solve the problem by sorting the array first. Sorting takes at least O(nlogn) time.

21.2 Java Solution

We can use a HashSet to add and remove elements. HashSet is implemented by using a hash table. Elements are not ordered. The add, remove and contains methods have constant time complexity O(1).

```java
public static int longestConsecutive(int[] num) {
    // if array is empty, return 0
    if (num.length == 0) {
        return 0;
    }

    Set<Integer> set = new HashSet<Integer>();
    int max = 1;

    for (int e : num)
        set.add(e);

    for (int e : num) {
        int left = e - 1;
        int right = e + 1;
        int count = 1;

        while (set.contains(left)) {
            count++;
            set.remove(left);
            left--;
        }

        while (set.contains(right)) {
            count++;
            set.remove(right);
            right++;
        }

        max = Math.max(count, max);
    }

    return max;
}
```

After an element is checked, it should be removed from the set. Otherwise, time complexity would be O(mn) in which m is the average length of all consecutive sequences.

To clearly see the time complexity, I suggest you use some simple examples and manually execute the program. For example, given an array 1,2,4,5,3, the program time is m. m is the length of longest consecutive sequence.

We do have an extreme case here: If n is number of elements, m is average length of consecutive sequence, and m==n, then the time complexity is $O(n^2)$. The reason is that in this case, no element is removed from the set each time. You can use this array to get the point: 1,3,5,7,9.

22 Valid Palindrome

Given a string, determine if it is a palindrome, considering only alphanumeric characters and ignoring cases.

For example, "Red rum, sir, is murder" is a palindrome, while "Programcreek is awesome" is not.

Note: Have you consider that the string might be empty? This is a good question to ask during an interview.

For the purpose of this problem, we define empty string as valid palindrome.

22.1 Thoughts

From start and end loop though the string, i.e., char array. If it is not alpha or number, increase or decrease pointers. Compare the alpha and numeric characters. The solution below is pretty straightforward.

22.2 Java Solution 1 - Naive

```java
public class Solution {

    public boolean isPalindrome(String s) {

        if(s == null) return false;
        if(s.length() < 2) return true;

        char[] charArray = s.toCharArray();
        int len = s.length();
```

22 Valid Palindrome

```
        int i=0;
        int j=len-1;

        while(i<j){
            char left, right;

            while(i<len-1 && !isAlpha(left) && !isNum(left)){
                i++;
                left = charArray[i];
            }

            while(j>0 && !isAlpha(right) && !isNum(right)){
                j--;
                right = charArray[j];
            }

            if(i >= j)
                break;

            left = charArray[i];
            right = charArray[j];

            if(!isSame(left, right)){
                return false;
            }

            i++;
            j--;
        }
        return true;
    }

    public boolean isAlpha(char a){
        if((a >= 'a' && a <= 'z') || (a >= 'A' && a <= 'Z')){
            return true;
        }else{
            return false;
        }
    }

    public boolean isNum(char a){
        if(a >= '0' && a <= '9'){
            return true;
        }else{
            return false;
        }
    }

    public boolean isSame(char a, char b){
```

22 Valid Palindrome

```java
        if(isNum(a) && isNum(b)){
            return a == b;
        }else if(Character.toLowerCase(a) == Character.toLowerCase(b)){
            return true;
        }else{
            return false;
        }
    }
}
```

22.3 Java Solution 2 - Using Stack

This solution removes the special characters first. (Thanks to Tia)

```java
public boolean isPalindrome(String s) {
  s = s.replaceAll("[^a-zA-Z0-9]", "").toLowerCase();

  int len = s.length();
  if (len < 2)
    return true;

  Stack<Character> stack = new Stack<Character>();

  int index = 0;
  while (index < len / 2) {
    stack.push(s.charAt(index));
    index++;
  }

  if (len % 2 == 1)
    index++;

  while (index < len) {
    if (stack.empty())
      return false;

    char temp = stack.pop();
    if (s.charAt(index) != temp)
      return false;
    else
      index++;
  }

  return true;
}
```

22.4 Java Solution 3 - Using Two Pointers

In the discussion below, April and Frank use two pointers to solve this problem. This solution looks really simple.

```java
public class ValidPalindrome {
  public static boolean isValidPalindrome(String s){
    if(s==null||s.length()==0) return false;

    s = s.replaceAll("[^a-zA-Z0-9]", "").toLowerCase();
    System.out.println(s);

    for(int i = 0; i < s.length() ; i++){
      if(s.charAt(i) != s.charAt(s.length() - 1 - i)){
        return false;
      }
    }

    return true;
  }

  public static void main(String[] args) {
    String str = "A man, a plan, a canal: Panama";

    System.out.println(isValidPalindrome(str));
  }
}
```

23 ZigZag Conversion

The string "PAYPALISHIRING" is written in a zigzag pattern on a given number of rows like this: (you may want to display this pattern in a fixed font for better legibility)

```
P   A   H   N
A P L S I I G
Y   I   R
```

And then read line by line: "PAHNAPLSIIGYIR" Write the a method convert("PAYPALISHIRING", 3) which returns "PAHNAPLSIIGYIR".

23.1 Java Solution

```java
public String convert(String s, int numRows) {
  if (numRows == 1)
```

```
    return s;

  StringBuilder sb = new StringBuilder();
  // step
  int step = 2 * numRows - 2;

  for (int i = 0; i < numRows; i++) {
    //first & last rows
    if (i == 0 || i == numRows - 1) {
      for (int j = i; j < s.length(); j = j + step) {
        sb.append(s.charAt(j));
      }
    //middle rows
    } else {
      int j = i;
      boolean flag = true;
      int step1 = 2 * (numRows - 1 - i);
      int step2 = step - step1;

      while (j < s.length()) {
        sb.append(s.charAt(j));
        if (flag)
          j = j + step1;
        else
          j = j + step2;
        flag = !flag;
      }
    }
  }

  return sb.toString();
}
```

24 Add Binary

Given two binary strings, return their sum (also a binary string).
For example, a = "11", b = "1", the return is "100".

24.1 Java Solution

Very simple, nothing special. Note how to convert a character to an int.

```
public String addBinary(String a, String b) {
  if(a==null || a.length()==0)
    return b;
```

```java
    if(b==null || b.length()==0)
        return a;
    
    int pa = a.length()-1;
    int pb = b.length()-1;
    
    int flag = 0;
    StringBuilder sb = new StringBuilder();
    while(pa >= 0 || pb >=0){
        int va = 0;
        int vb = 0;
        
        if(pa >= 0){
            va = a.charAt(pa)=='0'? 0 : 1;
            pa--;
        }
        if(pb >= 0){
            vb = b.charAt(pb)=='0'? 0: 1;
            pb--;
        }
        
        int sum = va + vb + flag;
        if(sum >= 2){
            sb.append(String.valueOf(sum-2));
            flag = 1;
        }else{
            flag = 0;
            sb.append(String.valueOf(sum));
        }
    }
    
    if(flag == 1){
        sb.append("1");
    }
    
    String reversed = sb.reverse().toString();
    return reversed;
}
```

25 Length of Last Word

Given a string s consists of upper/lower-case alphabets and empty space characters ' ', return the length of last word in the string. If the last word does not exist, return 0.

25.1 Java Solution

Very simple question. We just need a flag to mark the start of letters from the end. If a letter starts and the next character is not a letter, return the length.

```java
public int lengthOfLastWord(String s) {
    if(s==null || s.length() == 0)
        return 0;

    int result = 0;
    int len = s.length();

    boolean flag = false;
    for(int i=len-1; i>=0; i--){
        char c = s.charAt(i);
        if((c>='a' && c<='z') || (c>='A' && c<='Z')){
            flag = true;
            result++;
        }else{
            if(flag)
                return result;
        }
    }

    return result;
}
```

26 Triangle

Given a triangle, find the minimum path sum from top to bottom. Each step you may move to adjacent numbers on the row below.

For example, given the following triangle

```
[
    [2],
   [3,4],
  [6,5,7],
 [4,1,8,3]
]
```

The minimum path sum from top to bottom is 11 (i.e., 2 + 3 + 5 + 1 = 11).

Note: Bonus point if you are able to do this using only O(n) extra space, where n is the total number of rows in the triangle.

26.1 Top-Down Approach (Wrong Answer!)

This solution gets wrong answer! I will try to make it work later.

```java
public class Solution {
    public int minimumTotal(ArrayList<ArrayList<Integer>> triangle) {

        int[] temp = new int[triangle.size()];
        int minTotal = Integer.MAX_VALUE;

        for(int i=0; i< temp.length; i++){
            temp[i] = Integer.MAX_VALUE;
        }

        if (triangle.size() == 1) {
            return Math.min(minTotal, triangle.get(0).get(0));
        }

        int first = triangle.get(0).get(0);

        for (int i = 0; i < triangle.size() - 1; i++) {
            for (int j = 0; j <= i; j++) {

                int a, b;

                if(i==0 && j==0){
                    a = first + triangle.get(i + 1).get(j);
                    b = first + triangle.get(i + 1).get(j + 1);

                }else{
                    a = temp[j] + triangle.get(i + 1).get(j);
                    b = temp[j] + triangle.get(i + 1).get(j + 1);

                }

                temp[j] = Math.min(a, temp[j]);
                temp[j + 1] = Math.min(b, temp[j + 1]);
            }
        }

        for (int e : temp) {
            if (e < minTotal)
                minTotal = e;
        }

        return minTotal;
    }
}
```

26.2 Bottom-Up (Good Solution)

We can actually start from the bottom of the triangle.

```java
public int minimumTotal(ArrayList<ArrayList<Integer>> triangle) {
  int[] total = new int[triangle.size()];
  int l = triangle.size() - 1;

  for (int i = 0; i < triangle.get(l).size(); i++) {
    total[i] = triangle.get(l).get(i);
  }

  // iterate from last second row
  for (int i = triangle.size() - 2; i >= 0; i--) {
    for (int j = 0; j < triangle.get(i + 1).size() - 1; j++) {
      total[j] = triangle.get(i).get(j) + Math.min(total[j], total[j + 1]);
    }
  }

  return total[0];
}
```

27 Contains Duplicate

Given an array of integers, find if the array contains any duplicates. Your function should return true if any value appears at least twice in the array, and it should return false if every element is distinct.

27.1 Java Solution

```java
public boolean containsDuplicate(int[] nums) {
  if(nums==null || nums.length==0)
     return false;

  HashSet<Integer> set = new HashSet<Integer>();
  for(int i: nums){
    if(!set.add(i)){
       return true;
    }
  }

  return false;
}
```

28 Contains Duplicate II

Given an array of integers and an integer k, return true if and only if there are two distinct indices i and j in the array such that nums[i] = nums[j] and the difference between i and j is at most k.

28.1 Java Solution

```java
public boolean containsNearbyDuplicate(int[] nums, int k) {
   HashMap<Integer, Integer> map = new HashMap<Integer, Integer>();
   int min = Integer.MAX_VALUE;

   for(int i=0; i<nums.length; i++){
      if(map.containsKey(nums[i])){
         int preIndex = map.get(nums[i]);
         int gap = i-preIndex;
         min = Math.min(min, gap);
      }
      map.put(nums[i], i);
   }

   if(min <= k){
      return true;
   }else{
      return false;
   }
}
```

29 Remove Duplicates from Sorted Array

Given a sorted array, remove the duplicates in place such that each element appear only once and return the new length. Do not allocate extra space for another array, you must do this in place with constant memory.

For example, given input array A = [1,1,2], your function should return length = 2, and A is now [1,2].

29 Remove Duplicates from Sorted Array

29.1 Thoughts

The problem is pretty straightforward. It returns the length of array with unique elements, but the original array need to be changed also. This problem should be reviewed with Remove Duplicates from Sorted Array II.

29.2 Solution 1

```
// Manipulate original array
public static int removeDuplicatesNaive(int[] A) {
  if (A.length < 2)
    return A.length;

  int j = 0;
  int i = 1;

  while (i < A.length) {
    if (A[i] == A[j]) {
      i++;
    } else {
      j++;
      A[j] = A[i];
      i++;
    }
  }

  return j + 1;
}
```

This method returns the number of unique elements, but does not change the original array correctly. For example, if the input array is 1, 2, 2, 3, 3, the array will be changed to 1, 2, 3, 3, 3. The correct result should be 1, 2, 3. Because array's size can not be changed once created, there is no way we can return the original array with correct results.

29.3 Solution 2

```
// Create an array with all unique elements
public static int[] removeDuplicates(int[] A) {
  if (A.length < 2)
    return A;

  int j = 0;
  int i = 1;

  while (i < A.length) {
```

```java
        if (A[i] == A[j]) {
            i++;
        } else {
            j++;
            A[j] = A[i];
            i++;
        }
    }

    int[] B = Arrays.copyOf(A, j + 1);

    return B;
}

public static void main(String[] args) {
    int[] arr = { 1, 2, 2, 3, 3 };
    arr = removeDuplicates(arr);
    System.out.println(arr.length);
}
```

In this method, a new array is created and returned.

29.4 Solution 3

If we only want to count the number of unique elements, the following method is good enough.

```java
// Count the number of unique elements
public static int countUnique(int[] A) {
    int count = 0;
    for (int i = 0; i < A.length - 1; i++) {
        if (A[i] == A[i + 1]) {
            count++;
        }
    }
    return (A.length - count);
}

public static void main(String[] args) {
    int[] arr = { 1, 2, 2, 3, 3 };
    int size = countUnique(arr);
    System.out.println(size);
}
```

30 Remove Duplicates from Sorted Array II

Follow up for "Remove Duplicates": What if duplicates are allowed at most twice?

For example, given sorted array A = [1,1,1,2,2,3], your function should return length = 5, and A is now [1,1,2,2,3].

30.1 Naive Approach

Given the method signature "public int removeDuplicates(int[] A)", it seems that we should write a method that returns a integer and that's it. After typing the following solution:

```java
public class Solution {
   public int removeDuplicates(int[] A) {
      if(A == null || A.length == 0)
         return 0;

      int pre = A[0];
      boolean flag = false;
      int count = 0;

      for(int i=1; i<A.length; i++){
         int curr = A[i];

         if(curr == pre){
            if(!flag){
               flag = true;
               continue;
            }else{
               count++;
            }
         }else{
            pre = curr;
            flag = false;
         }
      }

      return A.length - count;
   }
}
```

Online Judge returns:

```
Submission Result: Wrong Answer
Input: [1,1,1,2]
Output: [1,1,1]
Expected: [1,1,2]
```

30 Remove Duplicates from Sorted Array II

So this problem also requires in-place array manipulation.

30.2 Correct Solution

We can not change the given array's size, so we only change the first k elements of the array which has duplicates removed.

```java
public class Solution {
  public int removeDuplicates(int[] A) {
    if (A == null || A.length == 0)
      return 0;

    int pre = A[0];
    boolean flag = false;
    int count = 0;

    // index for updating
    int o = 1;

    for (int i = 1; i < A.length; i++) {
      int curr = A[i];

      if (curr == pre) {
        if (!flag) {
          flag = true;
          A[o++] = curr;

          continue;
        } else {
          count++;
        }
      } else {
        pre = curr;
        A[o++] = curr;
        flag = false;
      }
    }

    return A.length - count;
  }
}
```

30.3 Better Solution

```java
public class Solution {
  public int removeDuplicates(int[] A) {
    if (A.length <= 2)
```

```
    return A.length;

  int prev = 1; // point to previous
  int curr = 2; // point to current

  while (curr < A.length) {
    if (A[curr] == A[prev] && A[curr] == A[prev - 1]) {
      curr++;
    } else {
      prev++;
      A[prev] = A[curr];
      curr++;
    }
  }

  return prev + 1;
  }
}
```

31 Longest Substring Without Repeating Characters

Given a string, find the length of the longest substring without repeating characters. For example, the longest substring without repeating letters for "abcabcbb" is "abc", which the length is 3. For "bbbbb" the longest substring is "b", with the length of 1.

31.1 Java Solution 1

The first solution is like the problem of "determine if a string has all unique characters" in CC 150. We can use a flag array to track the existing characters for the longest substring without repeating characters.

```java
public int lengthOfLongestSubstring(String s) {
  boolean[] flag = new boolean[256];

  int result = 0;
  int start = 0;
  char[] arr = s.toCharArray();

  for (int i = 0; i < arr.length; i++) {
    char current = arr[i];
    if (flag[current]) {
      result = Math.max(result, i - start);
```

31 Longest Substring Without Repeating Characters

```java
      // the loop update the new start point
      // and reset flag array
      // for example, abccab, when it comes to 2nd c,
      // it update start from 0 to 3, reset flag for a,b
      for (int k = start; k < i; k++) {
        if (arr[k] == current) {
          start = k + 1;
          break;
        }
        flag[arr[k]] = false;
      }
    } else {
      flag[current] = true;
    }
  }

  result = Math.max(arr.length - start, result);

  return result;
}
```

31.2 Java Solution 2

This solution is from Tia. It is easier to understand than the first solution.

The basic idea is using a hash table to track existing characters and their position. When a repeated character occurs, check from the previously repeated character. However, the time complexity is higher - $O(n^3)$.

```java
public static int lengthOfLongestSubstring(String s) {

  char[] arr = s.toCharArray();
  int pre = 0;

  HashMap<Character, Integer> map = new HashMap<Character, Integer>();

  for (int i = 0; i < arr.length; i++) {
    if (!map.containsKey(arr[i])) {
      map.put(arr[i], i);
    } else {
      pre = Math.max(pre, map.size());
      i = map.get(arr[i]);
      map.clear();
    }
  }

  return Math.max(pre, map.size());
}
```

Consider the following simple example.

abcda

When loop hits the second "a", the HashMap contains the following:

a 0
b 1
c 2
d 3

The index i is set to 0 and incremented by 1, so the loop start from second element again.

32 Longest Substring Which Contains 2 Unique Characters

This is a problem asked by Google.

Given a string, find the longest substring that contains only two unique characters. For example, given "abcbbbbcccbddddadacb", the longest substring that contains 2 unique character is "bcbbbbcccb".

32.1 Longest Substring Which Contains 2 Unique Characters

In this solution, a hashmap is used to track the right most index of 2 unique elements in the map. When a third character is being added to the map, the left pointer needs to move to the leftmost position in the map.

You can use "abac" to walk through this solution.

```java
public static String maxSubString2UniqueChars(String s) {
  int maxLen = 0;
  String maxSubstring = null;
  int m = 0;

  // declare a map to track the right most position of the two characters
  HashMap<Character, Integer> map = new HashMap<Character, Integer>();

  for (int i = 0; i < s.length(); i++) {
    char c = s.charAt(i);
    // if map contains 2 characters, process
    if (map.size() == 2 && !map.containsKey(c)) {
      if (i - m > maxLen) {
        maxLen = i - m;
```

060

32 Longest Substring Which Contains 2 Unique Characters

```java
      maxSubstring = s.substring(m, i);
    }

    // get the left most index for
    int leftMost = s.length();
    for (Entry<Character, Integer> entry : map.entrySet()) {
      if (entry.getValue() < leftMost) {
        leftMost = entry.getValue();
      }
    }

    m = leftMost + 1;
    map.remove(s.charAt(leftMost));
  }

  map.put(c, i);
}

if (map.size() == 2 && maxLen == 0) {
  return s;
}

return maxSubstring;
}
```

Now if this question is extended to be "the longest substring that contains k unique characters", what should we do? Apparently, the solution above is not scalable.

32.2 Naive Solution for K Unique Characters

The above solution can be extended to be a more general solution which would allow k distinct characters.

```java
public static String maxSubStringKUniqueChars(String s, int k) {
  int maxLen = 0;
  String maxSubstring = null;
  int m = 0;

  // declare a map to track the right most position of the two characters
  HashMap<Character, Integer> map = new HashMap<Character, Integer>();

  for (int i = 0; i < s.length(); i++) {
    char c = s.charAt(i);
    // if map contains 2 characters, process
    if (map.size() == k && !map.containsKey(c)) {
      if (i - m > maxLen) {
        maxLen = i - m;
        maxSubstring = s.substring(m, i);
      }
```

32 Longest Substring Which Contains 2 Unique Characters

```java
      int leftMost = s.length();
      for (Entry<Character, Integer> entry : map.entrySet()) {
        if (entry.getValue() < leftMost) {
          leftMost = entry.getValue();
        }
      }

      m = leftMost + 1;
      map.remove(s.charAt(leftMost));
    }

    map.put(c, i);
  }

  if (map.size() == k && maxLen == 0) {
    return s;
  }

  return maxSubstring;
}
```

The time is O(n*k). Can you get a better solution?

32.3 Better Solution for K Unique Characters

```java
public static String maxSubStringKUniqueChars(String s, int k) {
  //declare a counter
  HashMap<Character, Integer> map = new HashMap<Character, Integer>();
  int start = 0;
  int maxLen = 0;
  String maxSubstring = null;

  for (int i = 0; i < s.length(); i++) {
    //add each char to the counter
    char c = s.charAt(i);
    if(map.containsKey(c)){
      map.put(c, map.get(c)+1);
    }else{
      map.put(c, 1);
    }

    if(map.size() == k+1){
      //get maximum
      int range = i-start;
      if(range > maxLen){
        maxLen = range;
        maxSubstring = s.substring(start, i);
```

```
        }

      //move left cursor toward right, so that substring contains only k chars
      char first = s.charAt(start);
      while(map.size()>k){
        int count = map.get(first);
        if(count>1){
          map.put(first,count-1);
        }else{
          map.remove(first);
        }
        start++;
      }
    }
  }

  if (map.size() == k && maxLen == 0) {
    return s;
  }

  return maxSubstring;
}
```

Time is O(n).

33 Minimum Window Substring

Given a string S and a string T, find the minimum window in S which will contain all the characters in T in complexity O(n).

For example, S = "ADOBECODEBANC", T = "ABC", Minimum window is "BANC".

33.1 Java Solution

```
public String minWindow(String s, String t) {
   if(t.length()>s.length())
      return "";
   String result = "";

   //character counter for t
   HashMap<Character, Integer> target = new HashMap<Character, Integer>();
   for(int i=0; i<t.length(); i++){
      char c = t.charAt(i);
      if(target.containsKey(c)){
         target.put(c,target.get(c)+1);
      }else{
         target.put(c,1);
```

063

```java
        }
    }
    
    // character counter for s
    HashMap<Character, Integer> map = new HashMap<Character, Integer>();
    int left = 0;
    int minLen = s.length()+1;
    
    int count = 0; // the total of mapped characters
    
    for(int i=0; i<s.length(); i++){
        char c = s.charAt(i);
        
        if(target.containsKey(c)){
            if(map.containsKey(c)){
                if(map.get(c)<target.get(c)){
                    count++;
                }
                map.put(c,map.get(c)+1);
            }else{
                map.put(c,1);
                count++;
            }
        }
        
        if(count == t.length()){
            char sc = s.charAt(left);
            while (!map.containsKey(sc) || map.get(sc) > target.get(sc)) {
                if (map.containsKey(sc) && map.get(sc) > target.get(sc))
                    map.put(sc, map.get(sc) - 1);
                left++;
                sc = s.charAt(left);
            }
            
            if (i - left + 1 < minLen) {
                result = s.substring(left, i + 1);
                minLen = i - left + 1;
            }
        }
    }
    
    return result;
}
```

34 Reverse Words in a String

Given an input string, reverse the string word by word.
For example, given s = "the sky is blue", return "blue is sky the".

34.1 Java Solution

This problem is pretty straightforward. We first split the string to words array, and then iterate through the array and add each element to a new string. Note: StringBuilder should be used to avoid creating too many Strings. If the string is very long, using String is not scalable since String is immutable and too many objects will be created and garbage collected.

```java
class Solution {
  public String reverseWords(String s) {
    if (s == null || s.length() == 0) {
      return "";
    }

    // split to words by space
    String[] arr = s.split(" ");
    StringBuilder sb = new StringBuilder();
    for (int i = arr.length - 1; i >= 0; --i) {
      if (!arr[i].equals("")) {
        sb.append(arr[i]).append(" ");
      }
    }
    return sb.length() == 0 ? "" : sb.substring(0, sb.length() - 1);
  }
}
```

35 Find Minimum in Rotated Sorted Array

Suppose a sorted array is rotated at some pivot unknown to you beforehand. (i.e., 0 1 2 4 5 6 7 might become 4 5 6 7 0 1 2).
Find the minimum element. You may assume no duplicate exists in the array.

35.1 Thoughts

When we search something from a sorted array, binary search is almost a top choice. Binary search is efficient for sorted arrays.

This problems seems like a binary search, and the key is how to break the array to two parts, so that we only need to work on half of the array each time, i.e., when to select the left half and when to select the right half.

If we pick the middle element, we can compare the middle element with the left-end element. If middle is less than leftmost, the left half should be selected; if the middle is greater than the leftmost, the right half should be selected. Using simple recursion, this problem can be solve in time log(n).

In addition, in any rotated sorted array, the rightmost element should be less than the left-most element, otherwise, the sorted array is not rotated and we can simply pick the leftmost element as the minimum.

35.2 Java Solution

Define a helper function, otherwise, we will need to use Arrays.copyOfRange() function, which may be expensive for large arrays.

```java
public int findMin(int[] num) {
    return findMin(num, 0, num.length - 1);
}

public int findMin(int[] num, int left, int right) {
    if (left == right)
        return num[left];
    if ((right - left) == 1)
        return Math.min(num[left], num[right]);

    int middle = left + (right - left) / 2;

    // not rotated
    if (num[left] < num[right]) {
        return num[left];

    // go right side
    } else if (num[middle] > num[left]) {
        return findMin(num, middle, right);

    // go left side
    } else {
        return findMin(num, left, middle);
    }
}
```

36 Find Minimum in Rotated Sorted Array II

36.1 Problem

Follow up for "Find Minimum in Rotated Sorted Array": What if duplicates are allowed?

Would this affect the run-time complexity? How and why?

36.2 Java Solution

This is a follow-up problem of finding minimum element in rotated sorted array without duplicate elements. We only need to add one more condition, which checks if the left-most element and the right-most element are equal. If they are we can simply drop one of them. In my solution below, I drop the left element whenever the left-most equals to the right-most.

```java
public int findMin(int[] num) {
   return findMin(num, 0, num.length-1);
}

public int findMin(int[] num, int left, int right){
   if(right==left){
      return num[left];
   }
   if(right == left +1){
      return Math.min(num[left], num[right]);
   }
   // 3 3 1 3 3 3

   int middle = (right-left)/2 + left;
   // already sorted
   if(num[right] > num[left]){
      return num[left];
   //right shift one
   }else if(num[right] == num[left]){
      return findMin(num, left+1, right);
   //go right
   }else if(num[middle] >= num[left]){
      return findMin(num, middle, right);
   //go left
   }else{
      return findMin(num, left, middle);
   }
}
```

37 Find Peak Element

A peak element is an element that is greater than its neighbors. Given an input array where num[i] ≠ num[i+1], find a peak element and return its index. The array may contain multiple peaks, in that case return the index to any one of the peaks is fine.

You may imagine that num[-1] = num[n] = -∞. For example, in array [1, 2, 3, 1], 3 is a peak element and your function should return the index number 2.

37.1 Thoughts

This is a very simple problem. We can scan the array and find any element that is greater can its previous and next. The first and last element are handled separately.

37.2 Java Solution

```java
public class Solution {
    public int findPeakElement(int[] num) {
        int max = num[0];
        int index = 0;
        for(int i=1; i<=num.length-2; i++){
            int prev = num[i-1];
            int curr = num[i];
            int next = num[i+1];

            if(curr > prev && curr > next && curr > max){
                index = i;
                max = curr;
            }
        }

        if(num[num.length-1] > max){
            return num.length-1;
        }

        return index;
    }
}
```

38 Min Stack

Design a stack that supports push, pop, top, and retrieving the minimum element in constant time.

push(x) – Push element x onto stack. pop() – Removes the element on top of the stack. top() – Get the top element. getMin() – Retrieve the minimum element in the stack.

38.1 Thoughts

An array is a perfect fit for this problem. We can use a integer to track the top of the stack. You can use the Stack class from Java SDK, but I think a simple array is more efficient and more beautiful.

38.2 Java Solution

```java
class MinStack {
    private int[] arr = new int[100];
    private int index = -1;

    public void push(int x) {
        if(index == arr.length - 1){
            arr = Arrays.copyOf(arr, arr.length*2);
        }
        arr[++index] = x;
    }

    public void pop() {
        if(index>-1){
            if(index == arr.length/2 && arr.length > 100){
                arr = Arrays.copyOf(arr, arr.length/2);
            }
            index--;
        }
    }

    public int top() {
        if(index > -1){
            return arr[index];
        }else{
            return 0;
        }
    }

    public int getMin() {
        int min = Integer.MAX_VALUE;
        for(int i=0; i<=index; i++){
```

```java
        if(arr[i] < min)
            min = arr[i];
    }
    return min;
    }
}
```

39 Majority Element

Problem:

Given an array of size n, find the majority element. The majority element is the element that appears more than $\lfloor n/2 \rfloor$ times. You may assume that the array is non-empty and the majority element always exist in the array.

39.1 Java Solution 1

We can sort the array first, which takes time of nlog(n). Then scan once to find the longest consecutive substrings.

```java
public class Solution {
    public int majorityElement(int[] num) {
        if(num.length==1){
            return num[0];
        }

        Arrays.sort(num);

        int prev=num[0];
        int count=1;
        for(int i=1; i<num.length; i++){
            if(num[i] == prev){
                count++;
                if(count > num.length/2) return num[i];
            }else{
                count=1;
                prev = num[i];
            }
        }

        return 0;
    }
}
```

39.2 Java Solution 2 - Much Simpler

Thanks to SK. His/her solution is much efficient and simpler. Since the majority always take more than a half space, the middle element is guaranteed to be the majority. Sorting array takes nlog(n). So the time complexity of this solution is nlog(n). Cheers!

```java
public int majorityElement(int[] num) {
   if (num.length == 1) {
      return num[0];
   }

   Arrays.sort(num);
   return num[num.length / 2];
}
```

40 Remove Element

Given an array and a value, remove all instances of that value in place and return the new length. (Note: The order of elements can be changed. It doesn't matter what you leave beyond the new length.)

40.1 Java Solution

This problem can be solve by using two indices.

```java
public int removeElement(int[] A, int elem) {
   int i=0;
   int j=0;

   while(j < A.length){
      if(A[j] != elem){
         A[i] = A[j];
         i++;
      }

      j++;
   }

   return i;
}
```

41 Largest Rectangle in Histogram

Given n non-negative integers representing the histogram's bar height where the width of each bar is 1, find the area of largest rectangle in the histogram.

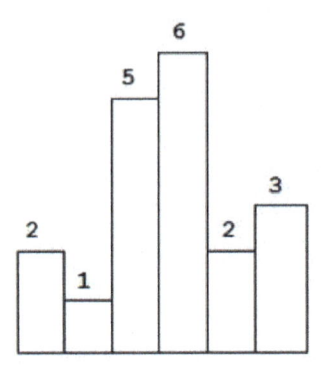

Above is a histogram where width of each bar is 1, given height = [2,1,5,6,2,3].

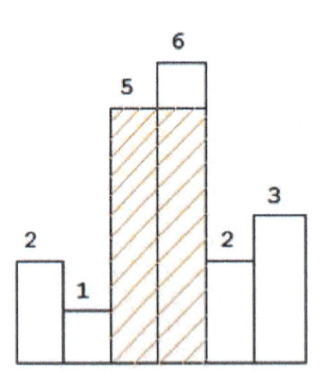

For example, given height = [2,1,5,6,2,3], return 10.

41.1 Analysis

The key to solve this problem is to maintain a stack to store bars' indexes. The stack only keeps the increasing bars.

41.2 Java Solution

```java
public int largestRectangleArea(int[] height) {
    if (height == null || height.length == 0) {
        return 0;
    }
```

```java
    Stack<Integer> stack = new Stack<Integer>();

    int max = 0;
    int i = 0;

    while (i < height.length) {
      //push index to stack when the current height is larger than the previous
          one
      if (stack.isEmpty() || height[i] >= height[stack.peek()]) {
        stack.push(i);
        i++;
      } else {
      //calculate max value when the current height is less than the previous
          one
        int p = stack.pop();
        int h = height[p];
        int w = stack.isEmpty() ? i : i - stack.peek() - 1;
        max = Math.max(h * w, max);
      }

    }

    while (!stack.isEmpty()) {
      int p = stack.pop();
      int h = height[p];
      int w = stack.isEmpty() ? i : i - stack.peek() - 1;
      max = Math.max(h * w, max);
    }

    return max;
}
```

42 Longest Common Prefix

42.1 Problem

Write a function to find the longest common prefix string amongst an array of strings.

42.2 Analysis

To solve this problem, we need to find the two loop conditions. One is the length of the shortest string. The other is iteration over every element of the string array.

42.3 Java Solution

```java
public String longestCommonPrefix(String[] strs) {
    if(strs == null || strs.length == 0)
        return "";

    int minLen=Integer.MAX_VALUE;
    for(String str: strs){
        if(minLen > str.length())
            minLen = str.length();
    }
    if(minLen == 0) return "";

    for(int j=0; j<minLen; j++){
        char prev='0';
        for(int i=0; i<strs.length ;i++){
            if(i==0) {
                prev = strs[i].charAt(j);
                continue;
            }

            if(strs[i].charAt(j) != prev){
                return strs[i].substring(0, j);
            }
        }
    }

    return strs[0].substring(0,minLen);
}
```

43 Largest Number

Given a list of non negative integers, arrange them such that they form the largest number.

For example, given [3, 30, 34, 5, 9], the largest formed number is 9534330. (Note: The result may be very large, so you need to return a string instead of an integer.)

43.1 Analysis

This problem can be solve by simply sorting strings, not sorting integer. Define a comparator to compare strings by concat() right-to-left or left-to-right.

43.2 Java Solution

```java
public String largestNumber(int[] num) {
    String[] NUM = new String[num.length];

    for (int i = 0; i <num.length; i++) {
       NUM[i] = String.valueOf(num[i]);
    }

    java.util.Arrays.sort(NUM, new java.util.Comparator<String>() {
       public int compare(String left, String right) {
          String leftRight = left.concat(right);
          String rightLeft = right.concat(left);
          return rightLeft.compareTo(leftRight);
       }
    });

    StringBuilder sb = new StringBuilder();
    for (int i = 0; i < NUM.length; i++) {
       sb.append(NUM[i]);
    }

    java.math.BigInteger result = new java.math.BigInteger(sb.toString());
    return result.toString();
}
```

44 Simplify Path

Given an absolute path for a file (Unix-style), simplify it.
For example,

```
path = "/home/",  => "/home"
path = "/a/./b/../../c/",  => "/c"
path = "/../",  => "/"
path = "/home//foo/",  => "/home/foo"
```

44.1 Java Solution

```java
public String simplifyPath(String path) {
    Stack<String> stack = new Stack<String>();

    //stack.push(path.substring(0,1));
```

```java
    while(path.length()> 0 && path.charAt(path.length()-1) =='/'){
        path = path.substring(0, path.length()-1);
    }
    
    int start = 0;
    for(int i=1; i<path.length(); i++){
        if(path.charAt(i) == '/'){
            stack.push(path.substring(start, i));
            start = i;
        }else if(i==path.length()-1){
            stack.push(path.substring(start));
        }
    }
    
    LinkedList<String> result = new LinkedList<String>();
    int back = 0;
    while(!stack.isEmpty()){
        String top = stack.pop();
        
        if(top.equals("/.") || top.equals("/")){
            //nothing
        }else if(top.equals("/..")){
            back++;
        }else{
            if(back > 0){
                back--;
            }else{
                result.push(top);
            }
        }
    }
    
    //if empty, return "/"
    if(result.isEmpty()){
        return "/";
    }
    
    StringBuilder sb = new StringBuilder();
    while(!result.isEmpty()){
        String s = result.pop();
        sb.append(s);
    }
    
    return sb.toString();
}
```

45 Compare Version Numbers

45.1 Problem

Compare two version numbers version1 and version2. If version1 >version2 return 1, if version1 <version2 return -1, otherwise return 0.

You may assume that the version strings are non-empty and contain only digits and the . character. The . character does not represent a decimal point and is used to separate number sequences.

Here is an example of version numbers ordering:

```
0.1 < 1.1 < 1.2 < 13.37
```

45.2 Java Solution

The tricky part of the problem is to handle cases like 1.0 and 1. They should be equal.

```java
public int compareVersion(String version1, String version2) {
    String[] arr1 = version1.split("\\.");
    String[] arr2 = version2.split("\\.");

    int i=0;
    while(i<arr1.length || i<arr2.length){
        if(i<arr1.length && i<arr2.length){
            if(Integer.parseInt(arr1[i]) < Integer.parseInt(arr2[i])){
                return -1;
            }else if(Integer.parseInt(arr1[i]) > Integer.parseInt(arr2[i])){
                return 1;
            }
        } else if(i<arr1.length){
            if(Integer.parseInt(arr1[i]) != 0){
                return 1;
            }
        } else if(i<arr2.length){
            if(Integer.parseInt(arr2[i]) != 0){
                return -1;
            }
        }

        i++;
    }

    return 0;
}
```

46 Gas Station

There are N gas stations along a circular route, where the amount of gas at station i is gas[i].

You have a car with an unlimited gas tank and it costs cost[i] of gas to travel from station i to its next station (i+1). You begin the journey with an empty tank at one of the gas stations.

Return the starting gas station's index if you can travel around the circuit once, otherwise return -1.

46.1 Analysis

To solve this problem, we need to understand and use the following 2 facts: 1) if the sum of gas >= the sum of cost, then the circle can be completed. 2) if A can not reach C in a the sequence of A–>B–>C, then B can not make it either.

Proof of fact 2:

```
If gas[A] < cost[A], then A can not even reach B.
So to reach C from A, gas[A] must >= cost[A].
Given that A can not reach C, we have gas[A] + gas[B] < cost[A] + cost[B],
and gas[A] >= cost[A],
Therefore, gas[B] < cost[B], i.e., B can not reach C.
```

In the following solution, sumRemaining tracks the sum of remaining to the current index. If sumRemaining <0, then every index between old start and current index is bad, and we need to update start to be the current index.

index	0	1	2	3	4
gas	1	2	3	4	5
cost	1	3	2	4	5

46.2 Java Solution

```java
public int canCompleteCircuit(int[] gas, int[] cost) {
  int sumRemaining = 0; // track current remaining
  int total = 0; // track total remaining
  int start = 0;
```

```java
  for (int i = 0; i < gas.length; i++) {
    int remaining = gas[i] - cost[i];

    //if sum remaining of (i-1) >= 0, continue
    if (sumRemaining >= 0) {
      sumRemaining += remaining;
    //otherwise, reset start index to be current
    } else {
      sumRemaining = remaining;
      start = i;
    }
    total += remaining;
  }

  if (total >= 0){
    return start;
  }else{
    return -1;
  }
}
```

47 Pascal's Triangle

Given numRows, generate the first numRows of Pascal's triangle. For example, given numRows = 5, the result should be:

```
[
    [1],
   [1,1],
  [1,2,1],
 [1,3,3,1],
[1,4,6,4,1]
]
```

47.1 Java Solution

```java
public ArrayList<ArrayList<Integer>> generate(int numRows) {
  ArrayList<ArrayList<Integer>> result = new ArrayList<ArrayList<Integer>>();
  if (numRows <= 0)
    return result;

  ArrayList<Integer> pre = new ArrayList<Integer>();
```

```java
    pre.add(1);
    result.add(pre);

    for (int i = 2; i <= numRows; i++) {
      ArrayList<Integer> cur = new ArrayList<Integer>();

      cur.add(1); //first
      for (int j = 0; j < pre.size() - 1; j++) {
        cur.add(pre.get(j) + pre.get(j + 1)); //middle
      }
      cur.add(1);//last

      result.add(cur);
      pre = cur;
    }

    return result;
}
```

48 Pascal's Triangle II

Given an index k, return the kth row of the Pascal's triangle. For example, when k = 3, the row is [1,3,3,1].

48.1 Analysis

This problem is related to Pascal's Triangle which gets all rows of Pascal's triangle. In this problem, only one row is required to return.

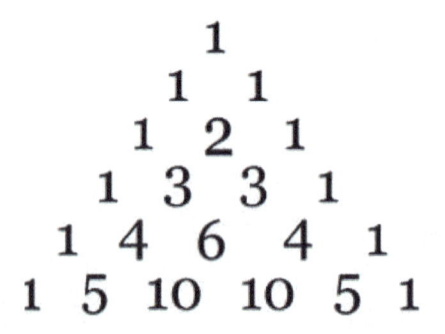

```
            1
          1   1
        1   2   1
      1   3   3   1
    1   4   6   4   1
  1   5  10  10   5   1
```

48.2 Java Solution

```java
public List<Integer> getRow(int rowIndex) {
  ArrayList<Integer> result = new ArrayList<Integer>();

  if (rowIndex < 0)
    return result;

  result.add(1);
  for (int i = 1; i <= rowIndex; i++) {
    for (int j = result.size() - 2; j >= 0; j--) {
      result.set(j + 1, result.get(j) + result.get(j + 1));
    }
    result.add(1);
  }
  return result;
}
```

49 Container With Most Water

49.1 Problem

Given n non-negative integers a1, a2, ..., an, where each represents a point at coordinate (i, ai). n vertical lines are drawn such that the two endpoints of line i is at (i, ai) and (i, 0). Find two lines, which together with x-axis forms a container, such that the container contains the most water.

49.2 Analysis

Initially we can assume the result is 0. Then we scan from both sides. If leftHeight <rightHeight, move right and find a value that is greater than leftHeight. Similarily, if leftHeight >rightHeight, move left and find a value that is greater than rightHeight. Additionally, keep tracking the max value.

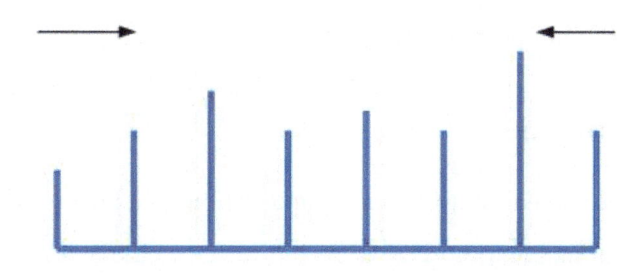

49.3 Java Solution

```java
public int maxArea(int[] height) {
  if (height == null || height.length < 2) {
    return 0;
  }

  int max = 0;
  int left = 0;
  int right = height.length - 1;

  while (left < right) {
    max = Math.max(max, (right - left) * Math.min(height[left],
        height[right]));
    if (height[left] < height[right])
      left++;
    else
      right--;
  }

  return max;
}
```

50 Count and Say

50.1 Problem

The count-and-say sequence is the sequence of integers beginning as follows: 1, 11, 21, 1211, 111221, ...

```
1 is read off as "one 1" or 11.
11 is read off as "two 1s" or 21.
21 is read off as "one 2, then one 1" or 1211.
```

Given an integer n, generate the nth sequence.

50.2 Java Solution

The problem can be solved by using a simple iteration. See Java solution below:

```java
public String countAndSay(int n) {
  if (n <= 0)
```

```java
    return null;

String result = "1";
int i = 1;

while (i < n) {
    StringBuilder sb = new StringBuilder();
    int count = 1;
    for (int j = 1; j < result.length(); j++) {
        if (result.charAt(j) == result.charAt(j - 1)) {
            count++;
        } else {
            sb.append(count);
            sb.append(result.charAt(j - 1));
            count = 1;
        }
    }

    sb.append(count);
    sb.append(result.charAt(result.length() - 1));
    result = sb.toString();
    i++;
}

return result;
}
```

51 Search for a Range

Given a sorted array of integers, find the starting and ending position of a given target value. Your algorithm's runtime complexity must be in the order of O(log n). If the target is not found in the array, return [-1, -1]. For example, given [5, 7, 7, 8, 8, 10] and target value 8, return [3, 4].

51.1 Java Solution

```java
public int[] searchRange(int[] nums, int target) {

    if(nums == null || nums.length == 0){
        return null;
    }

    ArrayList<Integer> result = new ArrayList<Integer>();
```

```
    for(int i=0; i< nums.length; i++){
        if(nums[i]==target){
            result.add(i);
        }
    }

    int[] arr = new int[2];

    if(result.size() == 0){
        arr[0]=-1;
        arr[1]=-1;
    }else{
        arr[0] = result.get(0);
        arr[1] = result.get(result.size()-1);
    }

    return arr;
}
```

52 Kth Largest Element in an Array

Find the kth largest element in an unsorted array. Note that it is the kth largest element in the sorted order, not the kth distinct element.

For example, given [3,2,1,5,6,4] and k = 2, return 5.

Note: You may assume k is always valid, $1 \leq k \leq$ array's length.

52.1 Java Solution 1

```
public int findKthLargest(int[] nums, int k) {
    Arrays.sort(nums);
    return nums[nums.length-k];
}
```

Time is O(nlog(n))

52.2 Java Solution 2

This problem can also be solve by using the quickselect approach, which is similar to quicksort.

```
public int findKthLargest(int[] nums, int k) {
    if (k < 1 || nums == null) {
        return 0;
```

```java
    }
    return getKth(nums.length - k +1, nums, 0, nums.length - 1);
}
public int getKth(int k, int[] nums, int start, int end) {
    int pivot = nums[end];

    int left = start;
    int right = end;

    while (true) {
        while (nums[left] < pivot && left < right) {
            left++;
        }

        while (nums[right] >= pivot && right > left) {
            right--;
        }

        if (left == right) {
            break;
        }

        swap(nums, left, right);
    }

    swap(nums, left, end);

    if (k == left + 1) {
        return pivot;
    } else if (k < left + 1) {
        return getKth(k, nums, start, left - 1);
    } else {
        return getKth(k, nums, left + 1, end);
    }
}
public void swap(int[] nums, int n1, int n2) {
    int tmp = nums[n1];
    nums[n1] = nums[n2];
    nums[n2] = tmp;
}
```

53 Anagrams

Given an array of strings, return all groups of strings that are anagrams.

53.1 Analysis

An anagram is a type of word play, the result of rearranging the letters of a word or phrase to produce a new word or phrase, using all the original letters exactly once; for example Torchwood can be rearranged into Doctor Who.

If two strings are anagram to each other, their sorted sequence is the same. Therefore, this problem can be seen as a problem of finding duplicate elements.

53.2 Java Solution

```java
public List<String> anagrams(String[] strs) {
    ArrayList<String> result = new ArrayList<String>();
    if(strs == null || strs.length == 0)
        return result;

    HashMap<String, ArrayList<Integer>> map = new HashMap<String,
        ArrayList<Integer>>();
    for(int i=0; i<strs.length; i++){
        char[] arr = strs[i].toCharArray();
        Arrays.sort(arr);
        String t = String.valueOf(arr);
        if(map.get(t) == null){
            ArrayList<Integer> l = new ArrayList<Integer>();
            l.add(i);
            map.put(t, l);
        }else{
            map.get(t).add(i);
        }
    }

    for(ArrayList<Integer> l: map.values()){
        if(l.size() > 1){
            for(Integer i: l){
                result.add(strs[i]);
            }
        }
    }

    return result;
```

Average case time is O(n), worst case time is O(n²).

}

54 First Missing Positive

Given an unsorted integer array, find the first missing positive integer. For example, given [1,2,0] return 3 and [3,4,-1,1] return 2.

Your algorithm should run in O(n) time and uses constant space.

54.1 Analysis

This problem can solve by using a bucket-sort like algorithm. Let's consider finding first missing positive and 0 first. The key fact is that the ith element should be i, so we have: i==A[i] A[i]==A[A[i]]

```
int firstMissingPositiveAnd0(int A[], int n) {
  for (int i = 0; i < n; i++) {
    // when the ith element is not i
    while (A[i] != i) {
      // no need to swap when ith element is out of range [0,n]
      if (A[i] < 0 || A[i] >= n)
        break;

      // swap elements
      int temp = A[i];
      A[i] = A[temp];
      A[temp] = temp;
    }
  }

  for (int i = 0; i < n; i++) {
    if (A[i] != i)
      return i;
  }

  return n;
}
```

54.2 Java Solution

This problem only considers positive numbers, so we need to shift 1 offset. The ith element is i+1.

```
int firstMissingPositive(int A[], int n) {
```

```
    for (int i = 0; i < n; i++) {
      while (A[i] != i + 1) {
        if (A[i] <= 0 || A[i] > n)
          break;

        int temp = A[i];
        A[i] = A[temp - 1];
        A[temp - 1] = temp;
      }
    }
    for (int i = 0; i < n; i++)
      if (A[i] != i + 1)
        return i + 1;
    return n + 1;
}
```

55 Shortest Palindrome

Given a string S, you are allowed to convert it to a palindrome by adding characters in front of it. Find and return the shortest palindrome you can find by performing this transformation.

For example, given "aacecaaa", return "aaacecaaa"; given "abcd", return "dcbabcd".

55.1 Analysis

We can solve this problem by using one of the methods which is used to solve the longest palindrome substring problem.

Specifically, we can start from the center and scan two sides. If read the left boundary, then the shortest palindrome is identified.

55.2 Java Solution

```
public String shortestPalindrome(String s) {
  if (s == null || s.length() <= 1)
    return s;

  String result = null;

  int len = s.length();
  int mid = len / 2;

  for (int i = mid; i >= 1; i--) {
```

```java
    if (s.charAt(i) == s.charAt(i - 1)) {
      if ((result = scanFromCenter(s, i - 1, i)) != null)
        return result;
    } else {
      if ((result = scanFromCenter(s, i - 1, i - 1)) != null)
        return result;
    }
  }

  return result;
}

private String scanFromCenter(String s, int l, int r) {
  int i = 1;

  //scan from center to both sides
  for (; l - i >= 0; i++) {
    if (s.charAt(l - i) != s.charAt(r + i))
      break;
  }

  //if not end at the beginning of s, return null
  if (l - i >= 0)
    return null;

  StringBuilder sb = new StringBuilder(s.substring(r + i));
  sb.reverse();

  return sb.append(s).toString();
}
```

56 Set Matrix Zeroes

Given a m x n matrix, if an element is 0, set its entire row and column to 0. Do it in place.

56.1 Thoughts about This Problem

This problem can solve by following 4 steps:

- check if first row and column are zero or not
- mark zeros on first row and column
- use mark to set elements

56 Set Matrix Zeroes

- set first column and row by using marks in step 1

56.2 Java Solution

```java
public class Solution {
    public void setZeroes(int[][] matrix) {
        boolean firstRowZero = false;
        boolean firstColumnZero = false;

        //set first row and column zero or not
        for(int i=0; i<matrix.length; i++){
            if(matrix[i][0] == 0){
                firstColumnZero = true;
                break;
            }
        }

        for(int i=0; i<matrix[0].length; i++){
            if(matrix[0][i] == 0){
                firstRowZero = true;
                break;
            }
        }

        //mark zeros on first row and column
        for(int i=1; i<matrix.length; i++){
            for(int j=1; j<matrix[0].length; j++){
                if(matrix[i][j] == 0){
                    matrix[i][0] = 0;
                    matrix[0][j] = 0;
                }
            }
        }

        //use mark to set elements
        for(int i=1; i<matrix.length; i++){
            for(int j=1; j<matrix[0].length; j++){
                if(matrix[i][0] == 0 || matrix[0][j] == 0){
                    matrix[i][j] = 0;
                }
            }
        }

        //set first column and row
        if(firstColumnZero){
            for(int i=0; i<matrix.length; i++)
                matrix[i][0] = 0;
        }
```

```java
        if(firstRowZero){
            for(int i=0; i<matrix[0].length; i++)
                matrix[0][i] = 0;
        }

    }
}
```

57 Spiral Matrix

Given a matrix of m x n elements (m rows, n columns), return all elements of the matrix in spiral order.

For example, given the following matrix:

```
[
 [ 1, 2, 3 ],
 [ 4, 5, 6 ],
 [ 7, 8, 9 ]
]
```

You should return [1,2,3,6,9,8,7,4,5].

57.1 Java Solution 1

If more than one row and column left, it can form a circle and we process the circle. Otherwise, if only one row or column left, we process that column or row ONLY.

```java
public class Solution {
    public ArrayList<Integer> spiralOrder(int[][] matrix) {
        ArrayList<Integer> result = new ArrayList<Integer>();

        if(matrix == null || matrix.length == 0) return result;

        int m = matrix.length;
        int n = matrix[0].length;

        int x=0;
        int y=0;

        while(m>0 && n>0){

            //if one row/column left, no circle can be formed
            if(m==1){
                for(int i=0; i<n; i++){
```

57 Spiral Matrix

```java
                result.add(matrix[x][y++]);
            }
            break;
        }else if(n==1){
            for(int i=0; i<m; i++){
                result.add(matrix[x++][y]);
            }
            break;
        }

        //below, process a circle

        //top - move right
        for(int i=0;i<n-1;i++){
            result.add(matrix[x][y++]);
        }

        //right - move down
        for(int i=0;i<m-1;i++){
            result.add(matrix[x++][y]);
        }

        //bottom - move left
        for(int i=0;i<n-1;i++){
            result.add(matrix[x][y--]);
        }

        //left - move up
        for(int i=0;i<m-1;i++){
            result.add(matrix[x--][y]);
        }

        x++;
        y++;
        m=m-2;
        n=n-2;
    }

    return result;
  }
}
```

57.2 Java Solution 2

We can also recursively solve this problem. The solution's performance is not better than Solution or as clear as Solution 1. Therefore, Solution 1 should be preferred.

```java
public class Solution {
```

57 Spiral Matrix

```java
public ArrayList<Integer> spiralOrder(int[][] matrix) {
    if(matrix==null || matrix.length==0)
        return new ArrayList<Integer>();
    
    return spiralOrder(matrix,0,0,matrix.length,matrix[0].length);
}


public ArrayList<Integer> spiralOrder(int [][] matrix, int x, int y, int
    m, int n){
    ArrayList<Integer> result = new ArrayList<Integer>();
    
    if(m<=0||n<=0)
        return result;
    
    //only one element left
    if(m==1&&n==1) {
        result.add(matrix[x][y]);
        return result;
    }
    
    //top - move right
    for(int i=0;i<n-1;i++){
        result.add(matrix[x][y++]);
    }
    
    //right - move down
    for(int i=0;i<m-1;i++){
        result.add(matrix[x++][y]);
    }
    
    //bottom - move left
    if(m>1){
        for(int i=0;i<n-1;i++){
            result.add(matrix[x][y--]);
        }
    }
    
    //left - move up
    if(n>1){
        for(int i=0;i<m-1;i++){
            result.add(matrix[x--][y]);
        }
    }
    
    if(m==1||n==1)
        result.addAll(spiralOrder(matrix, x, y, 1, 1));
    else
        result.addAll(spiralOrder(matrix, x+1, y+1, m-2, n-2));
```

```
        return result;
    }
}
```

58 Spiral Matrix II

Given an integer n, generate a square matrix filled with elements from 1 to n2 in spiral order. For example, given n = 4,

```
[
 [1,  2,  3, 4],
 [12, 13, 14, 5],
 [11, 16, 15, 6],
 [10, 9,  8, 7]
]
```

58.1 Java Solution

```java
public int[][] generateMatrix(int n) {
    int total = n*n;
    int[][] result= new int[n][n];

    int x=0;
    int y=0;
    int step = 0;

    for(int i=0;i<total;){
        while(y+step<n){
            i++;
            result[x][y]=i;
            y++;

        }
        y--;
        x++;

        while(x+step<n){
            i++;
            result[x][y]=i;
            x++;
        }
        x--;
        y--;
```

```
        while(y>=0+step){
            i++;
            result[x][y]=i;
            y--;
        }
        y++;
        x--;
        step++;

        while(x>=0+step){
            i++;
            result[x][y]=i;
            x--;
        }
        x++;
        y++;
    }

    return result;
}
```

59 Search a 2D Matrix

Write an efficient algorithm that searches for a value in an m x n matrix. This matrix has properties:

1) Integers in each row are sorted from left to right. 2) The first integer of each row is greater than the last integer of the previous row.

For example, consider the following matrix:

```
[
  [1,  3,  5,  7],
  [10, 11, 16, 20],
  [23, 30, 34, 50]
]
```

Given target = 3, return true.

59.1 Java Solution

This is a typical problem of binary search.

You may try to solve this problem by finding the row first and then the column. There is no need to do that. Because of the matrix's special features, the matrix can be considered as a sorted array. Your goal is to find one element in this sorted array by using binary search.

```java
public class Solution {
    public boolean searchMatrix(int[][] matrix, int target) {
        if(matrix==null || matrix.length==0 || matrix[0].length==0)
            return false;

        int m = matrix.length;
        int n = matrix[0].length;

        int start = 0;
        int end = m*n-1;

        while(start<=end){
            int mid=(start+end)/2;
            int midX=mid/n;
            int midY=mid%n;

            if(matrix[midX][midY]==target)
                return true;

            if(matrix[midX][midY]<target){
                start=mid+1;
            }else{
                end=mid-1;
            }
        }

        return false;
    }
}
```

60 Rotate Image

You are given an n x n 2D matrix representing an image.
Rotate the image by 90 degrees (clockwise).
Follow up: Could you do this in-place?

60.1 Naive Solution

In the following solution, a new 2-dimension array is created to store the rotated matrix, and the result is assigned to the matrix at the end. This is WRONG! Why?

```java
public class Solution {
    public void rotate(int[][] matrix) {
```

60 Rotate Image

```
        if(matrix == null || matrix.length==0)
           return ;
        
        int m = matrix.length;
        
        int[][] result = new int[m][m];
        
        for(int i=0; i<m; i++){
           for(int j=0; j<m; j++){
              result[j][m-1-i] = matrix[i][j];
           }
        }
        
        matrix = result;
    }
}
```

The problem is that Java is pass by value not by refrence! "matrix" is just a reference to a 2-dimension array. If "matrix" is assigned to a new 2-dimension array in the method, the original array does not change. Therefore, there should be another loop to assign each element to the array referenced by "matrix". Check out "Java pass by value."

```
public class Solution {
    public void rotate(int[][] matrix) {
        if(matrix == null || matrix.length==0)
           return ;
        
        int m = matrix.length;
        
        int[][] result = new int[m][m];
        
        for(int i=0; i<m; i++){
           for(int j=0; j<m; j++){
              result[j][m-1-i] = matrix[i][j];
           }
        }
        
        for(int i=0; i<m; i++){
           for(int j=0; j<m; j++){
              matrix[i][j] = result[i][j];
           }
        }
    }
}
```

60.2 In-place Solution

By using the relation "matrix[i][j] = matrix[n-1-j][i]", we can loop through the matrix.

```java
public void rotate(int[][] matrix) {
  int n = matrix.length;
  for (int i = 0; i < n / 2; i++) {
    for (int j = 0; j < Math.ceil(((double) n) / 2.); j++) {
      int temp = matrix[i][j];
      matrix[i][j] = matrix[n-1-j][i];
      matrix[n-1-j][i] = matrix[n-1-i][n-1-j];
      matrix[n-1-i][n-1-j] = matrix[j][n-1-i];
      matrix[j][n-1-i] = temp;
    }
  }
}
```

61 Valid Sudoku

Determine if a Sudoku is valid. The Sudoku board could be partially filled, where empty cells are filled with the character '.'.

61.1 Java Solution

```java
public boolean isValidSudoku(char[][] board) {
  if (board == null || board.length != 9 || board[0].length != 9)
    return false;
```

```java
  // check each column
  for (int i = 0; i < 9; i++) {
    boolean[] m = new boolean[9];
    for (int j = 0; j < 9; j++) {
      if (board[i][j] != '.') {
        if (m[(int) (board[i][j] - '1')]) {
          return false;
        }
        m[(int) (board[i][j] - '1')] = true;
      }
    }
  }

  //check each row
  for (int j = 0; j < 9; j++) {
    boolean[] m = new boolean[9];
    for (int i = 0; i < 9; i++) {
      if (board[i][j] != '.') {
        if (m[(int) (board[i][j] - '1')]) {
          return false;
        }
        m[(int) (board[i][j] - '1')] = true;
      }
    }
  }

  //check each 3*3 matrix
  for (int block = 0; block < 9; block++) {
    boolean[] m = new boolean[9];
    for (int i = block / 3 * 3; i < block / 3 * 3 + 3; i++) {
      for (int j = block % 3 * 3; j < block % 3 * 3 + 3; j++) {
        if (board[i][j] != '.') {
          if (m[(int) (board[i][j] - '1')]) {
            return false;
          }
          m[(int) (board[i][j] - '1')] = true;
        }
      }
    }
  }

  return true;
}
```

62 Minimum Path Sum

Given a m x n grid filled with non-negative numbers, find a path from top left to bottom right which minimizes the sum of all numbers along its path.

62.1 Java Solution 1: Depth-First Search

A native solution would be depth-first search. It's time is too expensive and fails the online judgement.

```java
public int minPathSum(int[][] grid) {
    return dfs(0,0,grid);
}

public int dfs(int i, int j, int[][] grid){
    if(i==grid.length-1 && j==grid[0].length-1){
        return grid[i][j];
    }

    if(i<grid.length-1 && j<grid[0].length-1){
        int r1 = grid[i][j] + dfs(i+1, j, grid);
        int r2 = grid[i][j] + dfs(i, j+1, grid);
        return Math.min(r1,r2);
    }

    if(i<grid.length-1){
        return grid[i][j] + dfs(i+1, j, grid);
    }

    if(j<grid[0].length-1){
        return grid[i][j] + dfs(i, j+1, grid);
    }

    return 0;
}
```

62.2 Java Solution 2: Dynamic Programming

```java
public int minPathSum(int[][] grid) {
    if(grid == null || grid.length==0)
        return 0;

    int m = grid.length;
    int n = grid[0].length;

    int[][] dp = new int[m][n];
    dp[0][0] = grid[0][0];
```

```java
    // initialize top row
    for(int i=1; i<n; i++){
        dp[0][i] = dp[0][i-1] + grid[0][i];
    }

    // initialize left column
    for(int j=1; j<m; j++){
        dp[j][0] = dp[j-1][0] + grid[j][0];
    }

    // fill up the dp table
    for(int i=1; i<m; i++){
        for(int j=1; j<n; j++){
            if(dp[i-1][j] > dp[i][j-1]){
                dp[i][j] = dp[i][j-1] + grid[i][j];
            }else{
                dp[i][j] = dp[i-1][j] + grid[i][j];
            }
        }
    }

    return dp[m-1][n-1];
}
```

63 Unique Paths

A robot is located at the top-left corner of a m x n grid. It can only move either down or right at any point in time. The robot is trying to reach the bottom-right corner of the grid.

How many possible unique paths are there?

63.1 Java Solution 1 - DFS

A depth-first search solution is pretty straight-forward. However, the time of this solution is too expensive, and it didn't pass the online judge.

```java
public int uniquePaths(int m, int n) {
    return dfs(0,0,m,n);
}

public int dfs(int i, int j, int m, int n){
    if(i==m-1 && j==n-1){
        return 1;
```

```java
    }

    if(i<m-1 && j<n-1){
        return dfs(i+1,j,m,n) + dfs(i,j+1,m,n);
    }

    if(i<m-1){
        return dfs(i+1,j,m,n);
    }

    if(j<n-1){
        return dfs(i,j+1,m,n);
    }

    return 0;
}
```

63.2 Java Solution 2 - Dynamic Programming

```java
public int uniquePaths(int m, int n) {
    if(m==0 || n==0) return 0;
    if(m==1 || n==1) return 1;

    int[][] dp = new int[m][n];

    //left column
    for(int i=0; i<m; i++){
        dp[i][0] = 1;
    }

    //top row
    for(int j=0; j<n; j++){
        dp[0][j] = 1;
    }

    //fill up the dp table
    for(int i=1; i<m; i++){
        for(int j=1; j<n; j++){
            dp[i][j] = dp[i-1][j] + dp[i][j-1];
        }
    }

    return dp[m-1][n-1];
}
```

64 Unique Paths II

Follow up for "Unique Paths":

Now consider if some obstacles are added to the grids. How many unique paths would there be?

An obstacle and empty space is marked as 1 and 0 respectively in the grid. For example, there is one obstacle in the middle of a 3x3 grid as illustrated below,

```
[
 [0,0,0],
 [0,1,0],
 [0,0,0]
]
```

the total number of unique paths is 2.

64.1 Java Solution

```java
public int uniquePathsWithObstacles(int[][] obstacleGrid) {
   if(obstacleGrid==null||obstacleGrid.length==0)
      return 0;

   int m = obstacleGrid.length;
   int n = obstacleGrid[0].length;

   if(obstacleGrid[0][0]==1||obstacleGrid[m-1][n-1]==1)
      return 0;


   int[][] dp = new int[m][n];
   dp[0][0]=1;

   //left column
   for(int i=1; i<m; i++){
      if(obstacleGrid[i][0]==1){
         dp[i][0] = 0;
      }else{
         dp[i][0] = dp[i-1][0];
      }
   }

   //top row
   for(int i=1; i<n; i++){
      if(obstacleGrid[0][i]==1){
```

```
            dp[0][i] = 0;
        }else{
            dp[0][i] = dp[0][i-1];
        }
    }
 
    //fill up cells inside
    for(int i=1; i<m; i++){
        for(int j=1; j<n; j++){
            if(obstacleGrid[i][j]==1){
                dp[i][j]=0;
            }else{
                dp[i][j]=dp[i-1][j]+dp[i][j-1];
            }
 
        }
    }
 
    return dp[m-1][n-1];
}
```

65 Number of Islands

Given a 2-d grid map of '1's (land) and '0's (water), count the number of islands. An island is surrounded by water and is formed by connecting adjacent lands horizontally or vertically. You may assume all four edges of the grid are all surrounded by water.

Example 1:

```
11110
11010
11000
00000
```

Answer: 1

Example 2:

```
11000
11000
00100
00011
```

Answer: 3

65.1 Java Solution

The basic idea of the following solution is merging adjacent lands, and the merging should be done recursively.

```java
public int numIslands(char[][] grid) {
   if (grid==null || grid.length==0 || grid[0].length==0) return 0;
   int count = 0;

   for (int i=0; i<grid.length; i++) {
      for (int j=0; j<grid[0].length; j++) {
         if(grid[i][j] == '1'){
            count++;
            merge(grid, i, j);
         }
      }
   }
   return count;
}

public void merge(char[][] grid, int i, int j){
   //validity checking
   if(i<0 || j<0 || i>grid.length-1 || j>grid[0].length-1)
      return;

   //if current cell is water or visited
   if(grid[i][j] != '1') return;

   //set visited cell to '2'
   grid[i][j] = '2';

   //merge all adjacent land
   merge(grid, i-1, j);
   merge(grid, i+1, j);
   merge(grid, i, j-1);
   merge(grid, i, j+1);
}
```

66 Surrounded Regions

Given a 2D board containing 'X' and 'O', capture all regions surrounded by 'X'. A region is captured by flipping all 'O's into 'X's in that surrounded region.

For example,

66 Surrounded Regions

```
X X X X
X O O X
X X O X
X O X X
```

After running your function, the board should be:

```
X X X X
X X X X
X X X X
X O X X
```

66.1 Analysis

This problem is similar to Number of Islands. In this problem, only the cells on the boarders can not be surrounded. So we can first merge those O's on the boarders like in Number of Islands and replace O's with '#', and then scan the board and replace all O's left (if any).

66.2 Depth-first Search

```java
public void solve(char[][] board) {
    if(board == null || board.length==0)
        return;

    int m = board.length;
    int n = board[0].length;

    //merge O's on left & right boarder
    for(int i=0;i<m;i++){
        if(board[i][0] == 'O'){
            merge(board, i, 0);
        }

        if(board[i][n-1] == 'O'){
            merge(board, i,n-1);
        }
    }

    //merge O's on top & bottom boarder
    for(int j=0; j<n; j++){
        if(board[0][j] == 'O'){
            merge(board, 0,j);
        }

        if(board[m-1][j] == 'O'){
            merge(board, m-1,j);
        }
    }
```

```java
        }

        //process the board
        for(int i=0;i<m;i++){
            for(int j=0; j<n; j++){
                if(board[i][j] == 'O'){
                    board[i][j] = 'X';
                }else if(board[i][j] == '#'){
                    board[i][j] = 'O';
                }
            }
        }
    }

    public void merge(char[][] board, int i, int j){
        if(i<0 || i>=board.length || j<0 || j>=board[0].length)
            return;

        if(board[i][j] != 'O')
            return;

        board[i][j] = '#';

        merge(board, i-1, j);
        merge(board, i+1, j);
        merge(board, i, j-1);
        merge(board, i, j+1);
    }
```

This solution causes java.lang.StackOverflowError, because for a large board, too many method calls are pushed to the stack and causes the overflow.

66.3 Breath-first Search

Instead we use a queue to do breath-first search.

```java
public class Solution {
    // use a queue to do BFS
    private Queue<Integer> queue = new LinkedList<Integer>();

    public void solve(char[][] board) {
        if (board == null || board.length == 0)
            return;

        int m = board.length;
        int n = board[0].length;

        // merge O's on left & right boarder
        for (int i = 0; i < m; i++) {
```

66 Surrounded Regions

```java
      if (board[i][0] == 'O') {
        bfs(board, i, 0);
      }

      if (board[i][n - 1] == 'O') {
        bfs(board, i, n - 1);
      }
    }

    // merge O's on top & bottom boarder
    for (int j = 0; j < n; j++) {
      if (board[0][j] == 'O') {
        bfs(board, 0, j);
      }

      if (board[m - 1][j] == 'O') {
        bfs(board, m - 1, j);
      }
    }

    // process the board
    for (int i = 0; i < m; i++) {
      for (int j = 0; j < n; j++) {
        if (board[i][j] == 'O') {
          board[i][j] = 'X';
        } else if (board[i][j] == '#') {
          board[i][j] = 'O';
        }
      }
    }
  }

  private void bfs(char[][] board, int i, int j) {
    int n = board[0].length;

    // fill current first and then its neighbors
    fillCell(board, i, j);

    while (!queue.isEmpty()) {
      int cur = queue.poll();
      int x = cur / n;
      int y = cur % n;

      fillCell(board, x - 1, y);
      fillCell(board, x + 1, y);
      fillCell(board, x, y - 1);
      fillCell(board, x, y + 1);
    }
  }
```

```java
    private void fillCell(char[][] board, int i, int j) {
        int m = board.length;
        int n = board[0].length;
        if (i < 0 || i >= m || j < 0 || j >= n || board[i][j] != 'O')
            return;

        // add current cell is queue & then process its neighbors in bfs
        queue.offer(i * n + j);
        board[i][j] = '#';
    }
}
```

67 Maximal Rectangle

Given a 2D binary matrix filled with 0's and 1's, find the largest rectangle containing all ones and return its area.

67.1 Analysis

This problem can be converted to the "Largest Rectangle in Histogram" problem.

67.2 Java Solution

```java
public int maximalRectangle(char[][] matrix) {
    int m = matrix.length;
    int n = m == 0 ? 0 : matrix[0].length;
    int[][] height = new int[m][n + 1];

    int maxArea = 0;
    for (int i = 0; i < m; i++) {
        for (int j = 0; j < n; j++) {
            if (matrix[i][j] == '0') {
                height[i][j] = 0;
            } else {
                height[i][j] = i == 0 ? 1 : height[i - 1][j] + 1;
            }
        }
    }

    for (int i = 0; i < m; i++) {
        int area = maxAreaInHist(height[i]);
        if (area > maxArea) {
            maxArea = area;
```

```java
      }
    }

    return maxArea;
}

private int maxAreaInHist(int[] height) {
    Stack<Integer> stack = new Stack<Integer>();

    int i = 0;
    int max = 0;

    while (i < height.length) {
      if (stack.isEmpty() || height[stack.peek()] <= height[i]) {
        stack.push(i++);
      } else {
        int t = stack.pop();
        max = Math.max(max, height[t]
            * (stack.isEmpty() ? i : i - stack.peek() - 1));
      }
    }

    return max;
}
```

---

68 Add Two Numbers

The problem:
> You are given two linked lists representing two non-negative numbers. The digits are stored in reverse order and each of their nodes contain a single digit. Add the two numbers and return it as a linked list. Input: (2 ->4 ->3) + (5 ->6 ->4) Output: 7 ->0 ->8

68.1 Thoughts

This is a simple problem. It can be solved by doing the following:

- Use a flag to mark if previous sum is >= 10
- Handle the situation that one list is longer than the other
- Correctly move the 3 pointers p1, p2 and p3 which pointer to two input lists and one output list

This leads to solution 1.

68.2 Solution 1

```java
// Definition for singly-linked list.
public class ListNode {
   int val;
   ListNode next;
   ListNode(int x) {
      val = x;
      next = null;
   }
}

public class Solution {
   public ListNode addTwoNumbers(ListNode l1, ListNode l2) {

      ListNode p1 = l1;
      ListNode p2 = l2;

      ListNode newHead = new ListNode(0);
      ListNode p3 = newHead;

      int val;//store sum

      boolean flag = false;//flag if greater than 10

      while(p1 != null || p2 != null){
         //both p1 and p2 have value
         if(p1 != null && p2 != null){

            if(flag){
               val = p1.val + p2.val + 1;
            }else{
               val = p1.val + p2.val;
            }

            //if sum >= 10
            if(val >= 10 ){
               flag = true;

            //if sum < 10
            }else{
               flag = false;
            }

            p3.next = new ListNode(val%10);
            p1 = p1.next;
            p2 = p2.next;
         //p1 is null, because p2 is longer
         }else if(p2 != null){
```

68 Add Two Numbers

```java
            if(flag){
                val = p2.val + 1;
                if(val >= 10){
                    flag = true;
                }else{
                    flag = false;
                }
            }else{
                val = p2.val;
                flag = false;
            }

            p3.next = new ListNode(val%10);
            p2 = p2.next;

        ////p2 is null, because p1 is longer
        }else if(p1 != null){

            if(flag){
                val = p1.val + 1;
                if(val >= 10){
                    flag = true;
                }else{
                    flag = false;
                }
            }else{
                val = p1.val;
                flag = false;
            }

            p3.next = new ListNode(val%10);
            p1 = p1.next;
        }

        p3 = p3.next;
    }

    //handle situation that same length final sum >=10
    if(p1 == null && p2 == null && flag){
        p3.next = new ListNode(1);
    }

    return newHead.next;
    }
}
```

The hard part is how to make the code more readable. Adding some internal comments and refactoring some code are helpful.

68.3 Solution 2

There is nothing wrong with solution 1, but the code is not readable. We can refactor the code and make it much shorter and cleaner.

```java
public class Solution {
    public ListNode addTwoNumbers(ListNode l1, ListNode l2) {
        int carry =0;

        ListNode newHead = new ListNode(0);
        ListNode p1 = l1, p2 = l2, p3=newHead;

        while(p1 != null || p2 != null){
            if(p1 != null){
                carry += p1.val;
                p1 = p1.next;
            }

            if(p2 != null){
                carry += p2.val;
                p2 = p2.next;
            }

            p3.next = new ListNode(carry%10);
            p3 = p3.next;
            carry /= 10;
        }

        if(carry==1)
            p3.next=new ListNode(1);

        return newHead.next;
    }
}
```

Exactly the same thing!

68.4 Quesion

What is the digits are stored in regular order instead of reversed order?

Answer: We can simple reverse the list, calculate the result, and reverse the result.

69 Reorder List

Given a singly linked list L: L0→L1→ ... →Ln-1→Ln, reorder it to: L0→Ln→L1→Ln-1→L2→Ln-2→...

For example, given 1,2,3,4, reorder it to 1,4,2,3. You must do this in-place without altering the nodes' values.

69.1 Analysis

This problem is not straightforward, because it requires "in-place" operations. That means we can only change their pointers, not creating a new list.

69.2 Java Solution

This problem can be solved by doing the following:

- Break list in the middle to two lists (use fast & slow pointers)
- Reverse the order of the second list
- Merge two list back together

The following code is a complete runnable class with testing.

```java
//Class definition of ListNode
class ListNode {
  int val;
  ListNode next;

  ListNode(int x) {
    val = x;
    next = null;
  }
}

public class ReorderList {

  public static void main(String[] args) {
    ListNode n1 = new ListNode(1);
    ListNode n2 = new ListNode(2);
    ListNode n3 = new ListNode(3);
    ListNode n4 = new ListNode(4);
    n1.next = n2;
    n2.next = n3;
```

69 Reorder List

```java
    n3.next = n4;

    printList(n1);

    reorderList(n1);

    printList(n1);
}

public static void reorderList(ListNode head) {

    if (head != null && head.next != null) {

        ListNode slow = head;
        ListNode fast = head;

        //use a fast and slow pointer to break the link to two parts.
        while (fast != null && fast.next != null && fast.next.next!= null) {
            //why need third/second condition?
            System.out.println("pre "+slow.val + " " + fast.val);
            slow = slow.next;
            fast = fast.next.next;
            System.out.println("after " + slow.val + " " + fast.val);
        }

        ListNode second = slow.next;
        slow.next = null;// need to close first part

        // now should have two lists: head and fast

        // reverse order for second part
        second = reverseOrder(second);

        ListNode p1 = head;
        ListNode p2 = second;

        //merge two lists here
        while (p2 != null) {
            ListNode temp1 = p1.next;
            ListNode temp2 = p2.next;

            p1.next = p2;
            p2.next = temp1;

            p1 = temp1;
            p2 = temp2;
        }
    }
}
```

69 Reorder List

```java
    public static ListNode reverseOrder(ListNode head) {

        if (head == null || head.next == null) {
            return head;
        }

        ListNode pre = head;
        ListNode curr = head.next;

        while (curr != null) {
            ListNode temp = curr.next;
            curr.next = pre;
            pre = curr;
            curr = temp;
        }

        // set head node's next
        head.next = null;

        return pre;
    }

    public static void printList(ListNode n) {
        System.out.println("------");
        while (n != null) {
            System.out.print(n.val);
            n = n.next;
        }
        System.out.println();
    }
}
```

69.3 Takeaway Messages

The three steps can be used to solve other problems of linked list. A little diagram may help better understand them.

Reverse List:

```
ListNode pre = head;
ListNode curr = head.next;

while (curr != null) {
        ListNode temp = curr.next;
        curr.next = pre;
        pre = curr;
        curr = temp;
}

head.next = null;
```

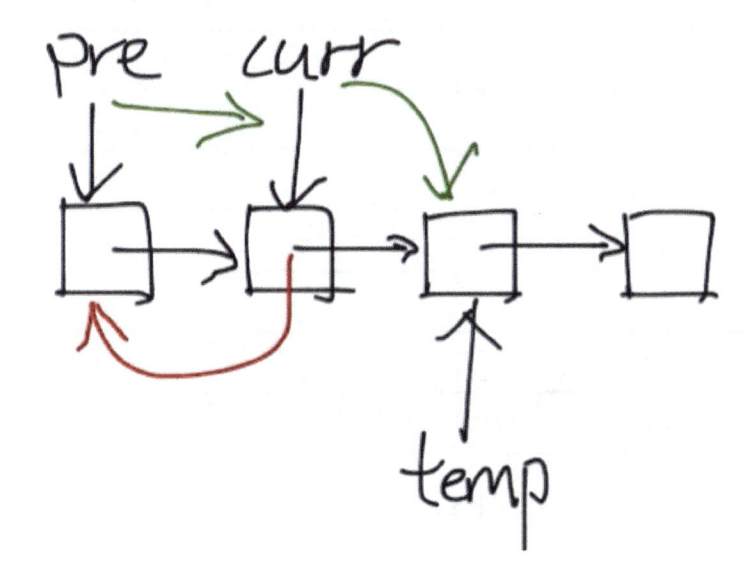

Merge List:

70 Linked List Cycle

```
ListNode p1 = head;
ListNode p2 = second;

//merge two lists here
while (p2 != null) {
        ListNode temp1 = p1.next;
        ListNode temp2 = p2.next;

        p1.next = p2;
        p2.next = temp1;

        p1 = temp1;
        p2 = temp2;
}
```

70 Linked List Cycle

Given a linked list, determine if it has a cycle in it.

70.1 Analysis

If we have 2 pointers - fast and slow. It is guaranteed that the fast one will meet the slow one if there exists a circle.

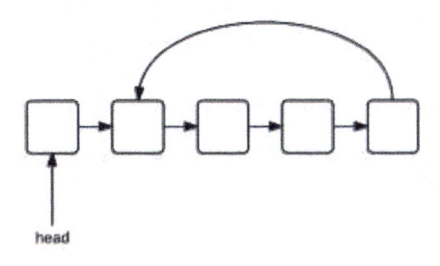

70.2 Java Solution

```java
public class Solution {
    public boolean hasCycle(ListNode head) {
        ListNode fast = head;
        ListNode slow = head;
        
        if(head == null)
            return false;
        
        if(head.next == null)
            return false;
        
        while(fast != null && fast.next != null){
            slow = slow.next;
            fast = fast.next.next;
            
            if(slow == fast)
                return true;
        }
        
        return false;
    }
}
```

71 Copy List with Random Pointer

A linked list is given such that each node contains an additional random pointer which could point to any node in the list or null.

Return a deep copy of the list.

71 Copy List with Random Pointer

71.1 Java Solution 1

We can solve this problem by doing the following steps:

- copy every node, i.e., duplicate every node, and insert it to the list
- copy random pointers for all newly created nodes
- break the list to two

```java
public RandomListNode copyRandomList(RandomListNode head) {

  if (head == null)
    return null;

  RandomListNode p = head;

  // copy every node and insert to list
  while (p != null) {
    RandomListNode copy = new RandomListNode(p.label);
    copy.next = p.next;
    p.next = copy;
    p = copy.next;
  }

  // copy random pointer for each new node
  p = head;
  while (p != null) {
    if (p.random != null)
      p.next.random = p.random.next;
    p = p.next.next;
  }

  // break list to two
  p = head;
  RandomListNode newHead = head.next;
  while (p != null) {
    RandomListNode temp = p.next;
    p.next = temp.next;
    if (temp.next != null)
      temp.next = temp.next.next;
    p = p.next;
  }

  return newHead;
}
```

The break list part above move pointer 2 steps each time, you can also move one at a time which is simpler, like the following:

```java
while(p != null && p.next != null){
```

```
    RandomListNode temp = p.next;
    p.next = temp.next;
    p = temp;
}
```

71.2 Java Solution 2 - Using HashMap

From Xiaomeng's comment below, we can use a HashMap which makes it simpler.

```
public RandomListNode copyRandomList(RandomListNode head) {
  if (head == null)
    return null;
  HashMap<RandomListNode, RandomListNode> map = new HashMap<RandomListNode,
      RandomListNode>();
  RandomListNode newHead = new RandomListNode(head.label);

  RandomListNode p = head;
  RandomListNode q = newHead;
  map.put(head, newHead);

  p = p.next;
  while (p != null) {
    RandomListNode temp = new RandomListNode(p.label);
    map.put(p, temp);
    q.next = temp;
    q = temp;
    p = p.next;
  }

  p = head;
  q = newHead;
  while (p != null) {
    if (p.random != null)
      q.random = map.get(p.random);
    else
      q.random = null;

    p = p.next;
    q = q.next;
  }

  return newHead;
}
```

72 Merge Two Sorted Lists

Merge two sorted linked lists and return it as a new list. The new list should be made by splicing together the nodes of the first two lists.

72.1 Analysis

The key to solve the problem is defining a fake head. Then compare the first elements from each list. Add the smaller one to the merged list. Finally, when one of them is empty, simply append it to the merged list, since it is already sorted.

72.2 Java Solution

```java
/**
 * Definition for singly-linked list.
 * public class ListNode {
 *     int val;
 *     ListNode next;
 *     ListNode(int x) {
 *         val = x;
 *         next = null;
 *     }
 * }
 */
public class Solution {
    public ListNode mergeTwoLists(ListNode l1, ListNode l2) {

        ListNode p1 = l1;
        ListNode p2 = l2;

        ListNode fakeHead = new ListNode(0);
        ListNode p = fakeHead;

        while(p1 != null && p2 != null){
          if(p1.val <= p2.val){
             p.next = p1;
             p1 = p1.next;
          }else{
             p.next = p2;
             p2 = p2.next;
          }

          p = p.next;
        }

        if(p1 != null)
           p.next = p1;
```

```
        if(p2 != null)
            p.next = p2;

        return fakeHead.next;
    }
}
```

73 Merge k Sorted Lists

Merge k sorted linked lists and return it as one sorted list. Analyze and describe its complexity.

73.1 Analysis

The simplest solution is using PriorityQueue. The elements of the priority queue are ordered according to their natural ordering, or by a comparator provided at the construction time (in this case).

73.2 Java Solution

```java
import java.util.ArrayList;
import java.util.Comparator;
import java.util.PriorityQueue;

// Definition for singly-linked list.
class ListNode {
    int val;
    ListNode next;

    ListNode(int x) {
        val = x;
        next = null;
    }
}

public class Solution {
    public ListNode mergeKLists(ArrayList<ListNode> lists) {
        if (lists.size() == 0)
            return null;

        //PriorityQueue is a sorted queue
        PriorityQueue<ListNode> q = new PriorityQueue<ListNode>(lists.size(),
            new Comparator<ListNode>() {
```

```java
      public int compare(ListNode a, ListNode b) {
        if (a.val > b.val)
          return 1;
        else if(a.val == b.val)
          return 0;
        else
          return -1;
      }
    });

    //add first node of each list to the queue
    for (ListNode list : lists) {
      if (list != null)
        q.add(list);
    }

    ListNode head = new ListNode(0);
    ListNode p = head; // serve as a pointer/cursor

    while (q.size() > 0) {
      ListNode temp = q.poll();
      //poll() retrieves and removes the head of the queue - q.
      p.next = temp;

      //keep adding next element of each list
      if (temp.next != null)
        q.add(temp.next);

      p = p.next;
    }

    return head.next;
  }
}
```

Time: log(k) * n. k is number of list and n is number of total elements.

74 Remove Duplicates from Sorted List

Given a sorted linked list, delete all duplicates such that each element appear only once.

For example,

Given 1->1->2, return 1->2.
Given 1->1->2->3->3, return 1->2->3.

74.1 Thoughts

The key of this problem is using the right loop condition. And change what is necessary in each loop. You can use different iteration conditions like the following 2 solutions.

74.2 Solution 1

```java
/**
 * Definition for singly-linked list.
 * public class ListNode {
 *     int val;
 *     ListNode next;
 *     ListNode(int x) {
 *         val = x;
 *         next = null;
 *     }
 * }
 */
public class Solution {
    public ListNode deleteDuplicates(ListNode head) {
        if(head == null || head.next == null)
            return head;

        ListNode prev = head;
        ListNode p = head.next;

        while(p != null){
            if(p.val == prev.val){
                prev.next = p.next;
                p = p.next;
                //no change prev
            }else{
                prev = p;
                p = p.next;
            }
        }

        return head;
    }
}
```

74.3 Solution 2

```java
public class Solution {
    public ListNode deleteDuplicates(ListNode head) {
        if(head == null || head.next == null)
            return head;

        ListNode p = head;

        while( p!= null && p.next != null){
            if(p.val == p.next.val){
                p.next = p.next.next;
            }else{
                p = p.next;
            }
        }

        return head;
    }
}
```

75 Partition List

Given a linked list and a value x, partition it such that all nodes less than x come before nodes greater than or equal to x.

You should preserve the original relative order of the nodes in each of the two partitions.

For example, Given 1->4->3->2->5->2 and x = 3, return 1->2->2->4->3->5.

75.1 Naive Solution (Wrong)

The following is a solution I write at the beginning. It contains a trivial problem, but it took me a long time to fix it.

```java
/**
 * Definition for singly-linked list.
 * public class ListNode {
 *     int val;
 *     ListNode next;
 *     ListNode(int x) {
 *         val = x;
 *         next = null;
 *     }
 * }
```

75 Partition List

```java
*/
public class Solution {
    public ListNode partition(ListNode head, int x) {
        if(head == null) return null;

        ListNode fakeHead1 = new ListNode(0);
        ListNode fakeHead2 = new ListNode(0);
        fakeHead1.next = head;

        ListNode p = head;
        ListNode prev = fakeHead1;
        ListNode p2 = fakeHead2;

        while(p != null){
            if(p.val < 3){
                p = p.next;
                prev = prev.next;
            }else{
                prev.next = p.next;
                p2.next = p;
                p = prev.next;
                p2 = p2.next;
            }
        }

        p.next = fakeHead2.next;
        return fakeHead1.next;
    }
}
```

75.2 Correct Solution

The problem of the first solution is that the last node's next element should be set to null.

```java
public class Solution {
    public ListNode partition(ListNode head, int x) {
        if(head == null) return null;

        ListNode fakeHead1 = new ListNode(0);
        ListNode fakeHead2 = new ListNode(0);
        fakeHead1.next = head;

        ListNode p = head;
        ListNode prev = fakeHead1;
        ListNode p2 = fakeHead2;

        while(p != null){
```

```java
            if(p.val < x){
                p = p.next;
                prev = prev.next;
            }else{

                p2.next = p;
                prev.next = p.next;

                p = prev.next;
                p2 = p2.next;
            }
        }

        // close the list
        p2.next = null;

        prev.next = fakeHead2.next;

        return fakeHead1.next;
    }
}
```

76 LRU Cache

76.1 Problem

Design and implement a data structure for Least Recently Used (LRU) cache. It should support the following operations: get and set.

get(key) - Get the value (will always be positive) of the key if the key exists in the cache, otherwise return -1. set(key, value) - Set or insert the value if the key is not already present. When the cache reached its capacity, it should invalidate the least recently used item before inserting a new item.

76.2 Java Solution

The key to solve this problem is using a double linked list which enables us to quickly move nodes.

76 LRU Cache

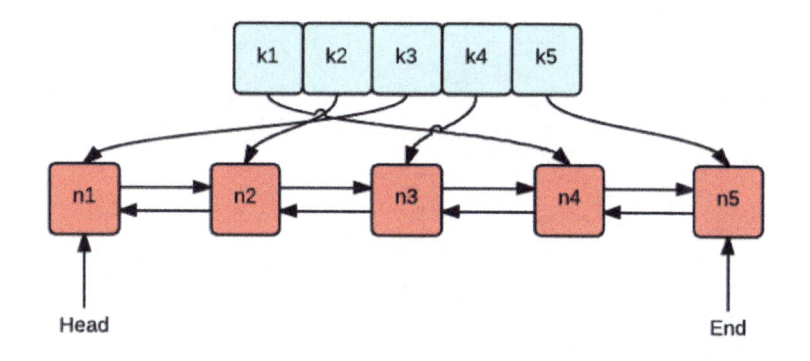

```
                k1  k2  k3  k4  k5


        n1  ←→  n2  ←→  n3  ←→  n4  ←→  n5
        ↑                               ↑
       Head                            End
```

```java
import java.util.HashMap;

public class LRUCache {
  private HashMap<Integer, DoubleLinkedListNode> map
    = new HashMap<Integer, DoubleLinkedListNode>();
  private DoubleLinkedListNode head;
  private DoubleLinkedListNode end;
  private int capacity;
  private int len;

  public LRUCache(int capacity) {
    this.capacity = capacity;
    len = 0;
  }

  public int get(int key) {
    if (map.containsKey(key)) {
      DoubleLinkedListNode latest = map.get(key);
      removeNode(latest);
      setHead(latest);
      return latest.val;
    } else {
      return -1;
    }
  }

  public void removeNode(DoubleLinkedListNode node) {
    DoubleLinkedListNode cur = node;
    DoubleLinkedListNode pre = cur.pre;
    DoubleLinkedListNode post = cur.next;

    if (pre != null) {
      pre.next = post;
    } else {
      head = post;
    }
```

76 LRU Cache

```java
      if (post != null) {
        post.pre = pre;
      } else {
        end = pre;
      }
    }

    public void setHead(DoubleLinkedListNode node) {
      node.next = head;
      node.pre = null;
      if (head != null) {
        head.pre = node;
      }

      head = node;
      if (end == null) {
        end = node;
      }
    }

    public void set(int key, int value) {
      if (map.containsKey(key)) {
        DoubleLinkedListNode oldNode = map.get(key);
        oldNode.val = value;
        removeNode(oldNode);
        setHead(oldNode);
      } else {
        DoubleLinkedListNode newNode =
          new DoubleLinkedListNode(key, value);
        if (len < capacity) {
          setHead(newNode);
          map.put(key, newNode);
          len++;
        } else {
          map.remove(end.key);
          end = end.pre;
          if (end != null) {
            end.next = null;
          }

          setHead(newNode);
          map.put(key, newNode);
        }
      }
    }
  }

  class DoubleLinkedListNode {
    public int val;
```

```
    public int key;
    public DoubleLinkedListNode pre;
    public DoubleLinkedListNode next;

    public DoubleLinkedListNode(int key, int value) {
        val = value;
        this.key = key;
    }
}
```

77 Intersection of Two Linked Lists

77.1 Problem

Write a program to find the node at which the intersection of two singly linked lists begins.

For example, the following two linked lists:

```
A:      a1 -> a2
                ->
                  c1 -> c2 -> c3
                ->
B:  b1 -> b2 -> b3
```

begin to intersect at node c1.

77.2 Java Solution

First calculate the length of two lists and find the difference. Then start from the longer list at the diff offset, iterate though 2 lists and find the node.

```java
/**
 * Definition for singly-linked list.
 * public class ListNode {
 *     int val;
 *     ListNode next;
 *     ListNode(int x) {
 *         val = x;
 *         next = null;
 *     }
 * }
 */
public class Solution {
```

```java
public ListNode getIntersectionNode(ListNode headA, ListNode headB) {
    int len1 = 0;
    int len2 = 0;
    ListNode p1=headA, p2=headB;
    if (p1 == null || p2 == null)
        return null;

    while(p1 != null){
        len1++;
        p1 = p1.next;
    }
    while(p2 !=null){
        len2++;
        p2 = p2.next;
    }

    int diff = 0;
    p1=headA;
    p2=headB;

    if(len1 > len2){
        diff = len1-len2;
        int i=0;
        while(i<diff){
            p1 = p1.next;
            i++;
        }
    }else{
        diff = len2-len1;
        int i=0;
        while(i<diff){
            p2 = p2.next;
            i++;
        }
    }

    while(p1 != null && p2 != null){
        if(p1.val == p2.val){
            return p1;
        }else{

        }
        p1 = p1.next;
        p2 = p2.next;
    }

    return null;
}
}
```

78 Remove Linked List Elements

Remove all elements from a linked list of integers that have value val.
Example

```
Given: 1 --> 2 --> 6 --> 3 --> 4 --> 5 --> 6, val = 6
Return: 1 --> 2 --> 3 --> 4 --> 5
```

78.1 Java Solution

The key to solve this problem is using a helper node to track the head of the list.

```java
public ListNode removeElements(ListNode head, int val) {
    ListNode helper = new ListNode(0);
    helper.next = head;
    ListNode p = helper;

    while(p.next != null){
        if(p.next.val == val){
            ListNode next = p.next;
            p.next = next.next;
        }else{
            p = p.next;
        }
    }

    return helper.next;
}
```

79 Swap Nodes in Pairs

Given a linked list, swap every two adjacent nodes and return its head.
For example, given 1->2->3->4, you should return the list as 2->1->4->3.
Your algorithm should use only constant space. You may not modify the values in the list, only nodes itself can be changed.

79.1 Java Solution

Use two template variable to track the previous and next node of each pair.

```java
public ListNode swapPairs(ListNode head) {
   if(head == null || head.next == null)
      return head;

   ListNode h = new ListNode(0);
   h.next = head;
   ListNode p = h;

   while(p.next != null && p.next.next != null){
      //use t1 to track first node
      ListNode t1 = p;
      p = p.next;
      t1.next = p.next;

      //use t2 to track next node of the pair
      ListNode t2 = p.next.next;
      p.next.next = p;
      p.next = t2;
   }

   return h.next;
}
```

80 Reverse Linked List

Reverse a singly linked list.

80.1 Java Solution 1 - Iterative

```java
public ListNode reverseList(ListNode head) {
   if(head==null || head.next == null)
      return head;

   ListNode p1 = head;
   ListNode p2 = head.next;

   head.next = null;
   while(p1!= null && p2!= null){
      ListNode t = p2.next;
      p2.next = p1;
      p1 = p2;
      if (t!=null){
         p2 = t;
```

```
        }else{
            break;
        }
    }

    return p2;
}
```

80.2 Java Solution 2 - Recursive

```java
public ListNode reverseList(ListNode head) {
    if(head==null || head.next == null)
        return head;

    //get second node
    ListNode second = head.next;
    //set first's next to be null
    head.next = null;

    ListNode rest = reverseList(second);
    second.next = head;

    return rest;
}
```

81 Remove Nth Node From End of List

Given a linked list, remove the nth node from the end of list and return its head.
For example, given linked list 1->2->3->4->5 and n = 2, the result is 1->2->3->5.

81.1 Java Solution 1 - Naive Two Passes

Calculate the length first, and then remove the nth from the beginning.

```java
public ListNode removeNthFromEnd(ListNode head, int n) {
    if(head == null)
        return null;

    //get length of list
    ListNode p = head;
    int len = 0;
    while(p != null){
```

81 Remove Nth Node From End of List

```
        len++;
        p = p.next;
    }

    //if remove first node
    int fromStart = len-n+1;
    if(fromStart==1)
        return head.next;

    //remove non-first node
    p = head;
    int i=0;
    while(p!=null){
        i++;
        if(i==fromStart-1){
            p.next = p.next.next;
        }
        p=p.next;
    }

    return head;
}
```

81.2 Java Solution 2 - One Pass

Use fast and slow pointers. The fast pointer is n steps ahead of the slow pointer. When the fast reaches the end, the slow pointer points at the previous element of the target element.

```
public ListNode removeNthFromEnd(ListNode head, int n) {
    if(head == null)
        return null;

    ListNode fast = head;
    ListNode slow = head;

    for(int i=0; i<n; i++){
        fast = fast.next;
    }

    //if remove the first node
    if(fast == null){
        head = head.next;
        return head;
    }

    while(fast.next != null){
        fast = fast.next;
```

```
    slow = slow.next;
  }

  slow.next = slow.next.next;

  return head;
}
```

82 Java PriorityQueue Class Example

In Java, the PriorityQueue class is implemented as a priority heap. Heap is an important data structure in computer science. For a quick overview of heap, here is a very good tutorial.

82.1 Simple Example

The following examples shows the basic operations of PriorityQueue such as offer(), peek(), poll(), and size().

```java
import java.util.Comparator;
import java.util.PriorityQueue;

public class PriorityQueueTest {

  static class PQsort implements Comparator<Integer> {

    public int compare(Integer one, Integer two) {
      return two - one;
    }
  }

  public static void main(String[] args) {
    int[] ia = { 1, 10, 5, 3, 4, 7, 6, 9, 8 };
    PriorityQueue<Integer> pq1 = new PriorityQueue<Integer>();

    // use offer() method to add elements to the PriorityQueue pq1
    for (int x : ia) {
      pq1.offer(x);
    }

    System.out.println("pq1: " + pq1);

    PQsort pqs = new PQsort();
    PriorityQueue<Integer> pq2 = new PriorityQueue<Integer>(10, pqs);
    // In this particular case, we can simply use Collections.reverseOrder()
```

```java
    // instead of self-defined comparator
    for (int x : ia) {
      pq2.offer(x);
    }

    System.out.println("pq2: " + pq2);

    // print size
    System.out.println("size: " + pq2.size());
    // return highest priority element in the queue without removing it
    System.out.println("peek: " + pq2.peek());
    // print size
    System.out.println("size: " + pq2.size());
    // return highest priority element and removes it from the queue
    System.out.println("poll: " + pq2.poll());
    // print size
    System.out.println("size: " + pq2.size());

    System.out.print("pq2: " + pq2);

  }
}
```

Output:

```
pq1: [1, 3, 5, 8, 4, 7, 6, 10, 9]
pq2: [10, 9, 7, 8, 3, 5, 6, 1, 4]
size: 9
peek: 10
size: 9
poll: 10
size: 8
pq2: [9, 8, 7, 4, 3, 5, 6, 1]
```

82.2 Example of Solving Problems Using PriorityQueue

Merging k sorted list.

For more details about PriorityQueue, please go to doc.

83 Solution for Binary Tree Preorder Traversal in Java

Preorder binary tree traversal is a classic interview problem about trees. The key to solve this problem is to understand the following:

- What is preorder? (parent node is processed before its children)
- Use Stack from Java Core library

It is not obvious what preorder for some strange cases. However, if you draw a stack and manually execute the program, how each element is pushed and popped is obvious.

The key to solve this problem is using a stack to store left and right children, and push right child first so that it is processed after the left child.

```java
public class TreeNode {
    int val;
    TreeNode left;
    TreeNode right;
    TreeNode(int x) { val = x; }
}

public class Solution {
    public ArrayList<Integer> preorderTraversal(TreeNode root) {
        ArrayList<Integer> returnList = new ArrayList<Integer>();

        if(root == null)
            return returnList;

        Stack<TreeNode> stack = new Stack<TreeNode>();
        stack.push(root);

        while(!stack.empty()){
            TreeNode n = stack.pop();
            returnList.add(n.val);

            if(n.right != null){
                stack.push(n.right);
            }
            if(n.left != null){
                stack.push(n.left);
            }
```

```java
        }
        return returnList;
    }
}
```

84 Solution of Binary Tree Inorder Traversal in Java

The key to solve inorder traversal of binary tree includes the following:
- The order of "inorder" is: left child ->parent ->right child
- Use a stack to track nodes
- Understand when to push node into the stack and when to pop node out of the stack

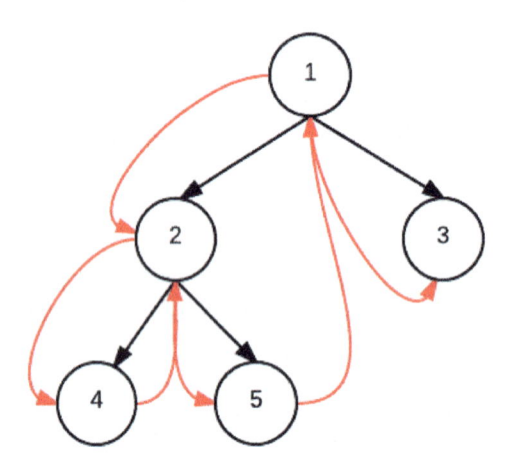

```java
//Definition for binary tree
public class TreeNode {
    int val;
    TreeNode left;
    TreeNode right;
    TreeNode(int x) { val = x; }
}

public class Solution {
    public ArrayList<Integer> inorderTraversal(TreeNode root) {
        // IMPORTANT: Please reset any member data you declared, as
```

```java
        // the same Solution instance will be reused for each test case.
         ArrayList<Integer> lst = new ArrayList<Integer>();
         
         if(root == null) 
            return lst;
            
         Stack<TreeNode> stack = new Stack<TreeNode>();
         //define a pointer to track nodes
         TreeNode p = root;
         
         while(!stack.empty() || p != null){
         
            // if it is not null, push to stack
            //and go down the tree to left
            if(p != null){
               stack.push(p);
               p = p.left;
               
            // if no left child
            // pop stack, process the node
            // then let p point to the right
            }else{
               TreeNode t = stack.pop();
               lst.add(t.val);
               p = t.right;
            }
         }
         
         return lst;
      }
}
```

85 Solution of Iterative Binary Tree Postorder Traversal in Java

The key to to iterative postorder traversal is the following:
- The order of "Postorder" is: left child ->right child ->parent node.
- Find the relation between the previously visited node and the current node
- Use a stack to track nodes

As we go down the tree, check the previously visited node. If it is the parent of the current node, we should add current node to stack. When there is no children

85 Solution of Iterative Binary Tree Postorder Traversal in Java

for current node, pop it from stack. Then the previous node become to be under the current node for next loop.

```java
//Definition for binary tree
public class TreeNode {
   int val;
   TreeNode left;
   TreeNode right;
   TreeNode(int x) { val = x; }
}


public class Solution {
   public ArrayList<Integer> postorderTraversal(TreeNode root) {

      ArrayList<Integer> lst = new ArrayList<Integer>();

      if(root == null)
         return lst;

      Stack<TreeNode> stack = new Stack<TreeNode>();
      stack.push(root);

      TreeNode prev = null;
      while(!stack.empty()){
         TreeNode curr = stack.peek();

         // go down the tree.
         //check if current node is leaf, if so, process it and pop stack,
         //otherwise, keep going down
         if(prev == null || prev.left == curr || prev.right == curr){
            //prev == null is the situation for the root node
            if(curr.left != null){
               stack.push(curr.left);
            }else if(curr.right != null){
               stack.push(curr.right);
            }else{
               stack.pop();
               lst.add(curr.val);
            }

         //go up the tree from left node
         //need to check if there is a right child
         //if yes, push it to stack
         //otherwise, process parent and pop stack
         }else if(curr.left == prev){
            if(curr.right != null){
               stack.push(curr.right);
            }else{
               stack.pop();
```

```java
            lst.add(curr.val);
        }

        //go up the tree from right node
        //after coming back from right node, process parent node and pop
            stack.
        }else if(curr.right == prev){
            stack.pop();
            lst.add(curr.val);
        }

        prev = curr;
    }

    return lst;
    }
}
```

86 Binary Tree Level Order Traversal

Given a binary tree, return the level order traversal of its nodes' values. (ie, from left to right, level by level).

For example: Given binary tree 3,9,20,#,#,15,7,

```
  3
 / \
9  20
  /  \
 15   7
```

return its level order traversal as [[3], [9,20], [15,7]]

86.1 Analysis

It is obvious that this problem can be solve by using a queue. However, if we use one queue we can not track when each level starts. So we use two queues to track the current level and the next level.

86.2 Java Solution

```java
public ArrayList<ArrayList<Integer>> levelOrder(TreeNode root) {
    ArrayList<ArrayList<Integer>> al = new ArrayList<ArrayList<Integer>>();
    ArrayList<Integer> nodeValues = new ArrayList<Integer>();
```

```java
    if(root == null)
       return al;

    LinkedList<TreeNode> current = new LinkedList<TreeNode>();
    LinkedList<TreeNode> next = new LinkedList<TreeNode>();
    current.add(root);

    while(!current.isEmpty()){
       TreeNode node = current.remove();

       if(node.left != null)
          next.add(node.left);
       if(node.right != null)
          next.add(node.right);

       nodeValues.add(node.val);
       if(current.isEmpty()){
          current = next;
          next = new LinkedList<TreeNode>();
          al.add(nodeValues);
          nodeValues = new ArrayList();
       }

    }
    return al;
}
```

87 Binary Tree Level Order Traversal II

Given a binary tree, return the bottom-up level order traversal of its nodes' values. For example, given binary tree 3,9,20,#,#,15,7,

```
3
 / \
9  20
   / \
  15  7
```

return its level order traversal as [[15,7], [9,20],[3]]

87.1 Java Solution

```java
public List<ArrayList<Integer>> levelOrderBottom(TreeNode root) {
   ArrayList<ArrayList<Integer>> result = new ArrayList<ArrayList<Integer>>();
```

```java
    if(root == null){
        return result;
    }

    LinkedList<TreeNode> current = new LinkedList<TreeNode>();
    LinkedList<TreeNode> next = new LinkedList<TreeNode>();
    current.offer(root);

    ArrayList<Integer> numberList = new ArrayList<Integer>();

    // need to track when each level starts
    while(!current.isEmpty()){
        TreeNode head = current.poll();

        numberList.add(head.val);

        if(head.left != null){
            next.offer(head.left);
        }
        if(head.right!= null){
            next.offer(head.right);
        }

        if(current.isEmpty()){
            current = next;
            next = new LinkedList<TreeNode>();
            result.add(numberList);
            numberList = new ArrayList<Integer>();
        }
    }

    //return Collections.reverse(result);
    ArrayList<ArrayList<Integer>> reversedResult = new
        ArrayList<ArrayList<Integer>>();
    for(int i=result.size()-1; i>=0; i--){
        reversedResult.add(result.get(i));
    }

    return reversedResult;
}
```

88 Validate Binary Search Tree

Problem:
Given a binary tree, determine if it is a valid binary search tree (BST).
Assume a BST is defined as follows:

- The left subtree of a node contains only nodes with keys less than the node's key.
- The right subtree of a node contains only nodes with keys greater than the node's key.
- Both the left and right subtrees must also be binary search trees.

88.1 Thoughts about This Problem

All values on the left sub tree must be less than root, and all values on the right sub tree must be greater than root.

88.2 Java Solution

```java
// Definition for binary tree
class TreeNode {
  int val;
  TreeNode left;
  TreeNode right;

  TreeNode(int x) {
    val = x;
  }
}

public class Solution {

  public static boolean isValidBST(TreeNode root) {
    return validate(root, Integer.MIN_VALUE, Integer.MAX_VALUE);
  }

  public static boolean validate(TreeNode root, int min, int max) {
    if (root == null) {
      return true;
    }

    // not in range
    if (root.val <= min || root.val >= max) {
      return false;
    }
```

```
        // left subtree must be < root.val && right subtree must be > root.val
        return validate(root.left, min, root.val) && validate(root.right,
            root.val, max);
    }
}
```

89 Flatten Binary Tree to Linked List

Given a binary tree, flatten it to a linked list in-place.
For example, Given

```
1
 / \
2   5
/ \   \
3  4   6
```

The flattened tree should look like:

```
1
 \
  2
   \
    3
     \
      4
       \
        5
         \
          6
```

89.1 Thoughts

Go down through the left, when right is not null, push right to stack.

89.2 Java Solution

```
/**
 * Definition for binary tree
 * public class TreeNode {
 *     int val;
 *     TreeNode left;
```

```java
 *     TreeNode right;
 *     TreeNode(int x) { val = x; }
 * }
 */
public class Solution {
    public void flatten(TreeNode root) {
        Stack<TreeNode> stack = new Stack<TreeNode>();
        TreeNode p = root;

        while(p != null || !stack.empty()){

            if(p.right != null){
                stack.push(p.right);
            }

            if(p.left != null){
                p.right = p.left;
                p.left = null;
            }else if(!stack.empty()){
                TreeNode temp = stack.pop();
                p.right=temp;
            }

            p = p.right;
        }
    }
}
```

90 Path Sum

Given a binary tree and a sum, determine if the tree has a root-to-leaf path such that adding up all the values along the path equals the given sum.

For example: Given the below binary tree and sum = 22,

```
5
 / \
4   8
/   / \
11 13  4
/ \     \
7  2     1
```

return true, as there exist a root-to-leaf path 5->4->11->2 which sum is 22.

90.1 Java Solution 1 - Using Queue

Add all node to a queue and store sum value of each node to another queue. When it is a leaf node, check the stored sum value.

For the tree above, the queue would be: 5 - 4 - 8 - 11 - 13 - 4 - 7 - 2 - 1. It will check node 13, 7, 2 and 1. This is a typical breadth first search(BFS) problem.

```java
/**
 * Definition for binary tree
 * public class TreeNode {
 *     int val;
 *     TreeNode left;
 *     TreeNode right;
 *     TreeNode(int x) { val = x; }
 * }
 */
public class Solution {
    public boolean hasPathSum(TreeNode root, int sum) {
        if(root == null) return false;

        LinkedList<TreeNode> nodes = new LinkedList<TreeNode>();
        LinkedList<Integer> values = new LinkedList<Integer>();

        nodes.add(root);
        values.add(root.val);

        while(!nodes.isEmpty()){
            TreeNode curr = nodes.poll();
            int sumValue = values.poll();

            if(curr.left == null && curr.right == null && sumValue==sum){
                return true;
            }

            if(curr.left != null){
                nodes.add(curr.left);
                values.add(sumValue+curr.left.val);
            }

            if(curr.right != null){
                nodes.add(curr.right);
                values.add(sumValue+curr.right.val);
            }
        }

        return false;
    }
}
```

90.2 Java Solution 2 - Recursion

```java
public boolean hasPathSum(TreeNode root, int sum) {
  if (root == null)
    return false;
  if (root.val == sum && (root.left == null && root.right == null))
    return true;

  return hasPathSum(root.left, sum - root.val)
      || hasPathSum(root.right, sum - root.val);
}
```

Thanks to nebulaliang, this solution is wonderful!

91 Path Sum II

Given a binary tree and a sum, find all root-to-leaf paths where each path's sum equals the given sum.

For example, given the below binary tree and sum = 22,

```
5
       / \
      4   8
     /   / \
    11  13  4
   / \    / \
  7   2  5   1
```

the method returns the following:

```
[
  [5,4,11,2],
  [5,8,4,5]
]
```

91.1 Analysis

This problem can be converted to be a typical depth-first search problem. A recursive depth-first search algorithm usually requires a recursive method call, a reference to the final result, a temporary result, etc.

91.2 Java Solution

```java
public List<ArrayList<Integer>> pathSum(TreeNode root, int sum) {
   ArrayList<ArrayList<Integer>> result = new ArrayList<ArrayList<Integer>>();
   if(root == null)
      return result;

   ArrayList<Integer> l = new ArrayList<Integer>();
   l.add(root.val);
   dfs(root, sum-root.val, result, l);
   return result;
}

public void dfs(TreeNode t, int sum, ArrayList<ArrayList<Integer>> result,
   ArrayList<Integer> l){
   if(t.left==null && t.right==null && sum==0){
      ArrayList<Integer> temp = new ArrayList<Integer>();
      temp.addAll(l);
      result.add(temp);
   }

   //search path of left node
   if(t.left != null){
      l.add(t.left.val);
      dfs(t.left, sum-t.left.val, result, l);
      l.remove(l.size()-1);
   }

   //search path of right node
   if(t.right!=null){
      l.add(t.right.val);
      dfs(t.right, sum-t.right.val, result, l);
      l.remove(l.size()-1);
   }
}
```

92 Construct Binary Tree from Inorder and Postorder Traversal

Given inorder and postorder traversal of a tree, construct the binary tree.

92 Construct Binary Tree from Inorder and Postorder Traversal

92.1 Throughts

This problem can be illustrated by using a simple example.

```
in-order:   4 2 5 (1) 6 7 3 8
post-order: 4 5 2 6 7 8 3 (1)
```

From the post-order array, we know that last element is the root. We can find the root in in-order array. Then we can identify the left and right sub-trees of the root from in-order array.

Using the length of left sub-tree, we can identify left and right sub-trees in post-order array. Recursively, we can build up the tree.

92.2 Java Solution

```java
//Definition for binary tree
public class TreeNode {
    int val;
    TreeNode left;
    TreeNode right;
    TreeNode(int x) { val = x; }
}

public class Solution {
    public TreeNode buildTree(int[] inorder, int[] postorder) {
        int inStart = 0;
        int inEnd = inorder.length-1;
        int postStart =0;
        int postEnd = postorder.length-1;

        return buildTree(inorder, inStart, inEnd, postorder, postStart,
            postEnd);
    }

    public TreeNode buildTree(int[] inorder, int inStart, int inEnd,
                  int[] postorder, int postStart, int postEnd){
        if(inStart > inEnd || postStart > postEnd)
            return null;

        int rootValue = postorder[postEnd];
        TreeNode root = new TreeNode(rootValue);

        int k=0;
        for(int i=0; i< inorder.length; i++){
            if(inorder[i]==rootValue){
                k = i;
                break;
            }
        }
```

```
        }
        root.left = buildTree(inorder, inStart, k-1, postorder, postStart,
            postStart+k-(inStart+1));
        // Becuase k is not the length, it it need to -(inStart+1) to get the
            length
        root.right = buildTree(inorder, k+1, inEnd, postorder,
            postStart+k-inStart, postEnd-1);
        // postStart+k-inStart = postStart+k-(inStart+1) +1

        return root;
    }
}
```

93 Convert Sorted Array to Binary Search Tree

Given an array where elements are sorted in ascending order, convert it to a height balanced BST.

93.1 Thoughts

Straightforward! Recursively do the job.

93.2 Java Solution

```
// Definition for binary tree
class TreeNode {
    int val;
    TreeNode left;
    TreeNode right;

    TreeNode(int x) {
        val = x;
    }
}

public class Solution {
    public TreeNode sortedArrayToBST(int[] num) {
        if (num.length == 0)
            return null;
```

```
    return sortedArrayToBST(num, 0, num.length - 1);
  }

  public TreeNode sortedArrayToBST(int[] num, int start, int end) {
    if (start > end)
      return null;

    int mid = (start + end) / 2;
    TreeNode root = new TreeNode(num[mid]);
    root.left = sortedArrayToBST(num, start, mid - 1);
    root.right = sortedArrayToBST(num, mid + 1, end);

    return root;
  }
}
```

94 Convert Sorted List to Binary Search Tree

Given a singly linked list where elements are sorted in ascending order, convert it to a height balanced BST.

94.1 Thoughts

If you are given an array, the problem is quite straightforward. But things get a little more complicated when you have a singly linked list instead of an array. Now you no longer have random access to an element in O(1) time. Therefore, you need to create nodes bottom-up, and assign them to its parents. The bottom-up approach enables us to access the list in its order at the same time as creating nodes.

94.2 Java Solution

```
// Definition for singly-linked list.
class ListNode {
  int val;
  ListNode next;

  ListNode(int x) {
    val = x;
    next = null;
  }
```

94 Convert Sorted List to Binary Search Tree

```java
}

// Definition for binary tree
class TreeNode {
  int val;
  TreeNode left;
  TreeNode right;

  TreeNode(int x) {
    val = x;
  }
}

public class Solution {
  static ListNode h;

  public TreeNode sortedListToBST(ListNode head) {
    if (head == null)
      return null;

    h = head;
    int len = getLength(head);
    return sortedListToBST(0, len - 1);
  }

  // get list length
  public int getLength(ListNode head) {
    int len = 0;
    ListNode p = head;

    while (p != null) {
      len++;
      p = p.next;
    }
    return len;
  }

  // build tree bottom-up
  public TreeNode sortedListToBST(int start, int end) {
    if (start > end)
      return null;

    // mid
    int mid = (start + end) / 2;

    TreeNode left = sortedListToBST(start, mid - 1);
    TreeNode root = new TreeNode(h.val);
    h = h.next;
    TreeNode right = sortedListToBST(mid + 1, end);
```

```
        root.left = left;
        root.right = right;

        return root;
    }
}
```

95 Minimum Depth of Binary Tree

Given a binary tree, find its minimum depth.
The minimum depth is the number of nodes along the shortest path from the root node down to the nearest leaf node.

95.1 Thoughts

Need to know LinkedList is a queue. add() and remove() are the two methods to manipulate the queue.

95.2 Java Solution

```java
/**
 * Definition for binary tree
 * public class TreeNode {
 *     int val;
 *     TreeNode left;
 *     TreeNode right;
 *     TreeNode(int x) { val = x; }
 * }
 */
public class Solution {
    public int minDepth(TreeNode root) {
        if(root == null){
            return 0;
        }

        LinkedList<TreeNode> nodes = new LinkedList<TreeNode>();
        LinkedList<Integer> counts = new LinkedList<Integer>();

        nodes.add(root);
        counts.add(1);

        while(!nodes.isEmpty()){
            TreeNode curr = nodes.remove();
```

```java
        int count = counts.remove();

        if(curr.left != null){
            nodes.add(curr.left);
            counts.add(count+1);
        }

        if(curr.right != null){
            nodes.add(curr.right);
            counts.add(count+1);
        }

        if(curr.left == null && curr.right == null){
            return count;
        }
    }

    return 0;
}
```

96 Binary Tree Maximum Path Sum

Given a binary tree, find the maximum path sum. The path may start and end at any node in the tree. For example, given the below binary tree

```
   1
  / \
 2   3
```

the result is 6.

96.1 Analysis

1) Recursively solve this problem 2) Get largest left sum and right sum 2) Compare to the stored maximum

96.2 Java Solution

We can also use an array to store value for recursive methods.

```java
public int maxPathSum(TreeNode root) {
    int max[] = new int[1];
    max[0] = Integer.MIN_VALUE;
```

```java
    calculateSum(root, max);
    return max[0];
}

public int calculateSum(TreeNode root, int[] max) {
    if (root == null)
        return 0;

    int left = calculateSum(root.left, max);
    int right = calculateSum(root.right, max);

    int current = Math.max(root.val, Math.max(root.val + left, root.val +
        right));

    max[0] = Math.max(max[0], Math.max(current, left + root.val + right));

    return current;
}
```

97 Balanced Binary Tree

Given a binary tree, determine if it is height-balanced.

For this problem, a height-balanced binary tree is defined as a binary tree in which the depth of the two subtrees of every node never differ by more than 1.

97.1 Thoughts

A typical recursive problem for solving tree problems.

97.2 Java Solution

```java
// Definition for binary tree
class TreeNode {
    int val;
    TreeNode left;
    TreeNode right;

    TreeNode(int x) {
        val = x;
    }
}

public class Solution {
```

```java
public boolean isBalanced(TreeNode root) {
  if (root == null)
    return true;

  if (getHeight(root) == -1)
    return false;

  return true;
}

public int getHeight(TreeNode root) {
  if (root == null)
    return 0;

  int left = getHeight(root.left);
  int right = getHeight(root.right);

  if (left == -1 || right == -1)
    return -1;

  if (Math.abs(left - right) > 1) {
    return -1;
  }

  return Math.max(left, right) + 1;

}
}
```

98 Symmetric Tree

98.1 Problem

Given a binary tree, check whether it is a mirror of itself (ie, symmetric around its center).

For example, this binary tree is symmetric:

```
1
 / \
2   2
/ \ / \
3 4 4 3
```

But the following is not:

```
   1
  / \
 2   2
  \   \
   3   3
```

98.2 Java Solution - Recursion

This problem can be solve by using a simple recursion. The key is finding the conditions that return false, such as value is not equal, only one node(left or right) has value.

```java
public boolean isSymmetric(TreeNode root) {
  if (root == null)
    return true;
  return isSymmetric(root.left, root.right);
}

public boolean isSymmetric(TreeNode l, TreeNode r) {
  if (l == null && r == null) {
    return true;
  } else if (r == null || l == null) {
    return false;
  }

  if (l.val != r.val)
    return false;

  if (!isSymmetric(l.left, r.right))
    return false;
  if (!isSymmetric(l.right, r.left))
    return false;

  return true;
}
```

99 Binary Search Tree Iterator

99 Binary Search Tree Iterator

99.1 Problem

Implement an iterator over a binary search tree (BST). Your iterator will be initialized with the root node of a BST. Calling next() will return the next smallest number in the BST. Note: next() and hasNext() should run in average O(1) time and uses O(h) memory, where h is the height of the tree.

99.2 Java Solution

The key to solve this problem is understanding what is BST. Here is a diagram.

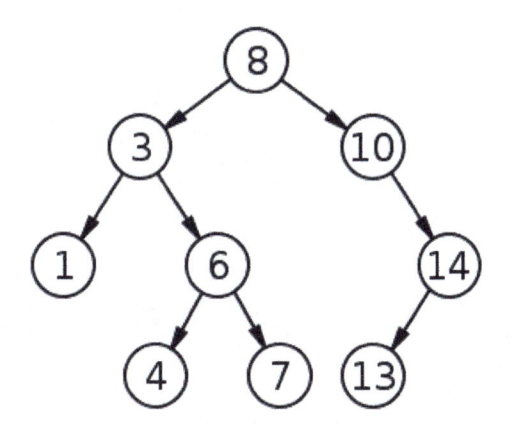

```
/**
 * Definition for binary tree
 * public class TreeNode {
 *     int val;
 *     TreeNode left;
 *     TreeNode right;
 *     TreeNode(int x) { val = x; }
 * }
 */
public class BSTIterator {
  Stack<TreeNode> stack;

  public BSTIterator(TreeNode root) {
    stack = new Stack<TreeNode>();
    while (root != null) {
      stack.push(root);
      root = root.left;
    }
  }

  public boolean hasNext() {
```

```java
    return !stack.isEmpty();
  }

  public int next() {
    TreeNode node = stack.pop();
    int result = node.val;
    if (node.right != null) {
      node = node.right;
      while (node != null) {
        stack.push(node);
        node = node.left;
      }
    }
    return result;
  }
}
```

100 Binary Tree Right Side View

Given a binary tree, imagine yourself standing on the right side of it, return the values of the nodes you can see ordered from top to bottom. For example, given the following binary tree,

```
1            <---
 / \
2   3        <---
 \
  5          <---
```

You can see [1, 3, 5].

100.1 Analysis

This problem can be solve by using a queue. On each level of the tree, we add the right-most element to the results.

100.2 Java Solution

```java
public List<Integer> rightSideView(TreeNode root) {
  ArrayList<Integer> result = new ArrayList<Integer>();

  if(root == null) return result;
```

```java
    LinkedList<TreeNode> queue = new LinkedList<TreeNode>();
    queue.add(root);

    while(queue.size() > 0){
        //get size here
        int size = queue.size();

        for(int i=0; i<size; i++){
            TreeNode top = queue.remove();

            //the first element in the queue (right-most of the tree)
            if(i==0){
                result.add(top.val);
            }
            //add right first
            if(top.right != null){
                queue.add(top.right);
            }
            //add left
            if(top.left != null){
                queue.add(top.left);
            }
        }
    }

    return result;
}
```

101 Implement Trie (Prefix Tree)

Implement a trie with insert, search, and startsWith methods.

101.1 Analysis

A trie node should contains the character, its children and the flag that marks if it is a leaf node.

101.2 Java Solution

You can use this diagram to walk though the Java solution.

101 Implement Trie (Prefix Tree)

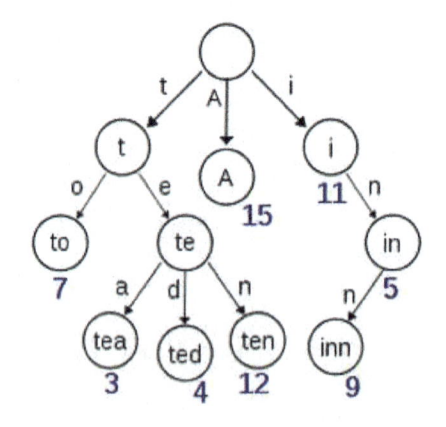

```
class TrieNode {
    char c;
    HashMap<Character, TrieNode> children = new HashMap<Character, TrieNode>();
    boolean isLeaf;

    public TrieNode() {}

    public TrieNode(char c){
        this.c = c;
    }
}
```

```
public class Trie {
    private TrieNode root;

    public Trie() {
        root = new TrieNode();
    }

    // Inserts a word into the trie.
    public void insert(String word) {
        HashMap<Character, TrieNode> children = root.children;

        for(int i=0; i<word.length(); i++){
            char c = word.charAt(i);

            TrieNode t;
            if(children.containsKey(c)){
                t = children.get(c);
            }else{
                t = new TrieNode(c);
                children.put(c, t);
            }
```

```java
            children = t.children;

            //set leaf node
            if(i==word.length()-1)
                t.isLeaf = true;
        }
    }

    // Returns if the word is in the trie.
    public boolean search(String word) {
        TrieNode t = searchNode(word);

        if(t != null && t.isLeaf)
            return true;
        else
            return false;
    }

    // Returns if there is any word in the trie
    // that starts with the given prefix.
    public boolean startsWith(String prefix) {
        if(searchNode(prefix) == null)
            return false;
        else
            return true;
    }

    public TrieNode searchNode(String str){
        Map<Character, TrieNode> children = root.children;
        TrieNode t = null;
        for(int i=0; i<str.length(); i++){
            char c = str.charAt(i);
            if(children.containsKey(c)){
                t = children.get(c);
                children = t.children;
            }else{
                return null;
            }
        }

        return t;
    }
}
```

102 Add and Search Word Data structure design

Design a data structure that supports the following two operations:

```
void addWord(word)
bool search(word)
```

search(word) can search a literal word or a regular expression string containing only letters a-z or .. A . means it can represent any one letter.

102.1 Analysis

This problem is similar with Implement Trie. The solution 1 below uses the same definition of a trie node. To handle the "." case for this problem, we need to search all possible paths, instead of one path.

102.2 Java Solution 1

TrieNode

```java
class TrieNode{
    char c;
    HashMap<Character, TrieNode> children = new HashMap<Character, TrieNode>();
    boolean isLeaf;

    public TrieNode() {}

    public TrieNode(char c){
        this.c = c;
    }
}
```

WordDictionary

```java
public class WordDictionary {
    private TrieNode root;

    public WordDictionary(){
        root = new TrieNode();
    }

    // Adds a word into the data structure.
    public void addWord(String word) {
        HashMap<Character, TrieNode> children = root.children;

        for(int i=0; i<word.length(); i++){
```

102 Add and Search Word Data structure design

```java
            char c = word.charAt(i);

            TrieNode t = null;
            if(children.containsKey(c)){
               t = children.get(c);
            }else{
               t = new TrieNode(c);
               children.put(c,t);
            }

            children = t.children;

            if(i == word.length()-1){
               t.isLeaf = true;
            }
        }
    }

    // Returns if the word is in the data structure. A word could
    // contain the dot character '.' to represent any one letter.
    public boolean search(String word) {
       return dfsSearch(root.children, word, 0);

    }

    public boolean dfsSearch(HashMap<Character, TrieNode> children, String
          word, int start) {
        if(start == word.length()){
           if(children.size()==0)
              return true;
           else
              return false;
        }

        char c = word.charAt(start);

        if(children.containsKey(c)){
           if(start == word.length()-1 && children.get(c).isLeaf){
              return true;
           }

           return dfsSearch(children.get(c).children, word, start+1);
        }else if(c == '.'){
           boolean result = false;
           for(Map.Entry<Character, TrieNode> child: children.entrySet()){
              if(start == word.length()-1 && child.getValue().isLeaf){
                 return true;
              }

              //if any path is true, set result to be true;
```

```
            if(dfsSearch(child.getValue().children, word, start+1)){
                result = true;
            }
        }

        return result;
    }else{
       return false;
    }
  }
}
```

103 Merge K Sorted Arrays in Java

This is a classic interview question. Another similar problem is "merge k sorted lists".

This problem can be solved by using a heap. The time is O(nlog(n)).

Given m arrays, the minimum elements of all arrays can form a heap. It takes O(log(m)) to insert an element to the heap and it takes O(1) to delete the minimum element.

```java
class ArrayContainer implements Comparable<ArrayContainer> {
  int[] arr;
  int index;

  public ArrayContainer(int[] arr, int index) {
    this.arr = arr;
    this.index = index;
  }

  @Override
  public int compareTo(ArrayContainer o) {
    if (this.arr[this.index] > o.arr[o.index]) {
      return 1;
    } else if (this.arr[this.index] < o.arr[o.index]) {
      return -1;
    } else {
      return 0;
    }
  }
}
```

```java
public class KSortedArray {
```

```java
public static int[] mergeKSortedArray(int[][] arr) {
    //PriorityQueue is heap in Java
    PriorityQueue<ArrayContainer> queue = new PriorityQueue<ArrayContainer>();
    int total=0;

    //add arrays to heap
    for (int i = 0; i < arr.length; i++) {
        queue.add(new ArrayContainer(arr[i], 0));
        total = total + arr[i].length;
    }

    int m=0;
    int result[] = new int[total];

    //while heap is not empty
    while(!queue.isEmpty()){
        ArrayContainer ac = queue.poll();
        result[m++]=ac.arr[ac.index];

        if(ac.index < ac.arr.length-1){
            queue.add(new ArrayContainer(ac.arr, ac.index+1));
        }
    }

    return result;
}

public static void main(String[] args) {
    int[] arr1 = { 1, 3, 5, 7 };
    int[] arr2 = { 2, 4, 6, 8 };
    int[] arr3 = { 0, 9, 10, 11 };

    int[] result = mergeKSortedArray(new int[][] { arr1, arr2, arr3 });
    System.out.println(Arrays.toString(result));
}
}
```

104 Populating Next Right Pointers in Each Node

Given the following perfect binary tree,

1

104 Populating Next Right Pointers in Each Node

```
    / \
   2   3
  / \ / \
 4  5 6  7
```

After calling your function, the tree should look like:

```
1 -> NULL
    / \
   2 -> 3 -> NULL
  / \ / \
 4->5->6->7 -> NULL
```

104.1 Java Solution 1

This solution is easier to understand. you can use the example tree above to walk through the algorithm. The basic idea is have two pointers(top and p) to move towards right on two levels.

```java
public void connect(TreeLinkNode root) {
    TreeLinkNode top = root;//the previous level, just use a better name for
        root
    while(top != null){
        TreeLinkNode levelFirst = null;//first of each level
        TreeLinkNode p = null;//cursor for node on each level

        while(top != null){
            //record the firston each level
            if(levelFirst == null){
                levelFirst = top.left;
            }

            if(top.left!=null){
                if(p!=null)
                    p.next = top.left;
                p=top.left;
            }
            if(top.right!=null){
                if(p!=null)
                    p.next = top.right;
                p = top.right;
            }

            top = top.next;
        }

        top = levelFirst;
    }
}
```

104.2 Java Solution 2

```java
public void connect(TreeLinkNode root) {
  if (root == null)
    return;

  //top node
  TreeLinkNode top = root;
  //first node of each level
  TreeLinkNode first = root.left;

   TreeLinkNode current = root;
  current.next = null;

  while (top != null && top.left != null) {
    while (top != null) {
      current = top.left;
      current.next = top.right;
      current = current.next;
      top = top.next;
      current.next = top == null ? null : top.left;
    }

    top = first;
    first = top == null ? null : top.left;
  }
}
```

105 Unique Binary Search Trees

Given n, how many structurally unique BST's (binary search trees) that store values 1...n?

For example, Given n = 3, there are a total of 5 unique BST's.

```
1         3     3      2      1
 \       /     /      / \      \
  3     2     1      1   3      2
 /     /       \                 \
2     1         2                 3
```

105.1 Analysis

Let count[i] be the number of unique binary search trees for i. The number of trees are determined by the number of subtrees which have different root node. For example,

```
i=0, count[0]=1 //empty tree

i=1, count[1]=1 //one tree

i=2, count[2]=count[0]*count[1] // 0 is root
        + count[1]*count[0] // 1 is root

i=3, count[3]=count[0]*count[2] // 1 is root
        + count[1]*count[1] // 2 is root
        + count[2]*count[0] // 3 is root

i=4, count[4]=count[0]*count[3] // 1 is root
        + count[1]*count[2] // 2 is root
        + count[2]*count[1] // 3 is root
        + count[3]*count[0] // 4 is root
..
..
..

i=n, count[n] = sum(count[0..k]*count[k+1...n]) 0 <= k < n-1
```

Use dynamic programming to solve the problem.

105.2 Java Solution

```java
public int numTrees(int n) {
  int[] count = new int[n + 1];

  count[0] = 1;
  count[1] = 1;

  for (int i = 2; i <= n; i++) {
    for (int j = 0; j <= i - 1; j++) {
      count[i] = count[i] + count[j] * count[i - j - 1];
    }
  }

  return count[n];
}
```

106 Unique Binary Search Trees II

Check out how to get all unique binary search trees.

Given n, generate all structurally unique BST's (binary search trees) that store values 1...n.

For example, Given n = 3, your program should return all 5 unique BST's shown below.

```
1         3     3      2      1
 \       /     /      / \      \
  3     2     1      1   3      2
 /     /       \                 \
2     1         2                 3
```

106.1 Analysis

Check out Unique Binary Search Trees I.

This problem can be solved by recursively forming left and right subtrees. The different combinations of left and right subtrees form the set of all unique binary search trees.

106.2 Java Solution

```java
public List<TreeNode> generateTrees(int n) {
   return generateTrees(1, n);
}

public List<TreeNode> generateTrees(int start, int end) {
   List<TreeNode> list = new LinkedList<>();

   if (start > end) {
      list.add(null);
      return list;
   }

   for (int i = start; i <= end; i++) {
      List<TreeNode> lefts = generateTrees(start, i - 1);
      List<TreeNode> rights = generateTrees(i + 1, end);
      for (TreeNode left : lefts) {
         for (TreeNode right : rights) {
            TreeNode node = new TreeNode(i);
```

```
            node.left = left;
            node.right = right;
            list.add(node);
        }
      }
   }

   return list;
}
```

107 Sum Root to Leaf Numbers

Given a binary tree containing digits from 0-9 only, each root-to-leaf path could represent a number. Find the total sum of all root-to-leaf numbers.
For example,

```
  1
 / \
2   3
```

The root-to-leaf path 1->2 represents the number 12. The root-to-leaf path 1->3 represents the number 13. Return the sum = 12 + 13 = 25.

107.1 Java Solution - Recursive

This problem can be solved by a typical DFS approach.

```java
public int sumNumbers(TreeNode root) {
   int result = 0;
   if(root==null)
      return result;

   ArrayList<ArrayList<TreeNode>> all = new ArrayList<ArrayList<TreeNode>>();
   ArrayList<TreeNode> l = new ArrayList<TreeNode>();
   l.add(root);
   dfs(root, l, all);

   for(ArrayList<TreeNode> a: all){
      StringBuilder sb = new StringBuilder();
      for(TreeNode n: a){
         sb.append(String.valueOf(n.val));
      }
      int currValue = Integer.valueOf(sb.toString());
      result = result + currValue;
   }
```

```java
      return result;
   }

   public void dfs(TreeNode n, ArrayList<TreeNode> l,
      ArrayList<ArrayList<TreeNode>> all){
      if(n.left==null && n.right==null){
         ArrayList<TreeNode> t = new ArrayList<TreeNode>();
         t.addAll(l);
         all.add(t);
      }

      if(n.left!=null){
         l.add(n.left);
         dfs(n.left, l, all);
         l.remove(l.size()-1);
      }

      if(n.right!=null){
         l.add(n.right);
         dfs(n.right, l, all);
         l.remove(l.size()-1);
      }

   }
```

Same approach, but simpler coding style.

```java
public int sumNumbers(TreeNode root) {
   if(root == null)
      return 0;

   return dfs(root, 0, 0);
}

public int dfs(TreeNode node, int num, int sum){
   if(node == null) return sum;

   num = num*10 + node.val;

   // leaf
   if(node.left == null && node.right == null) {
      sum += num;
      return sum;
   }

   // left subtree + right subtree
   sum = dfs(node.left, num, sum) + dfs(node.right, num, sum);
   return sum;
}
```

108 Clone Graph Java

LeetCode Problem:

Clone an undirected graph. Each node in the graph contains a label and a list of its neighbors.

OJ's undirected graph serialization:

Nodes are labeled uniquely.

We use `#` as a separator for each node, and `,` as a separator for node label and each neighbor of the node.

As an example, consider the serialized graph `{0,1,2#1,2#2,2}`.

The graph has a total of three nodes, and therefore contains three parts as separated by `#`.

1. First node is labeled as `0`. Connect node `0` to both nodes `1` and `2`.
2. Second node is labeled as `1`. Connect node `1` to node `2`.
3. Third node is labeled as `2`. Connect node `2` to node `2` (itself), thus forming a self-cycle.

Visually, the graph looks like the following:

```
    1
   / \
  /   \
 0 --- 2
      / \
      \_/
```

108.1 Key to Solve This Problem

- A queue is used to do breath first traversal.
- a map is used to store the visited nodes. It is the map between original node and copied node.

It would be helpful if you draw a diagram and visualize the problem.

108 Clone Graph Java

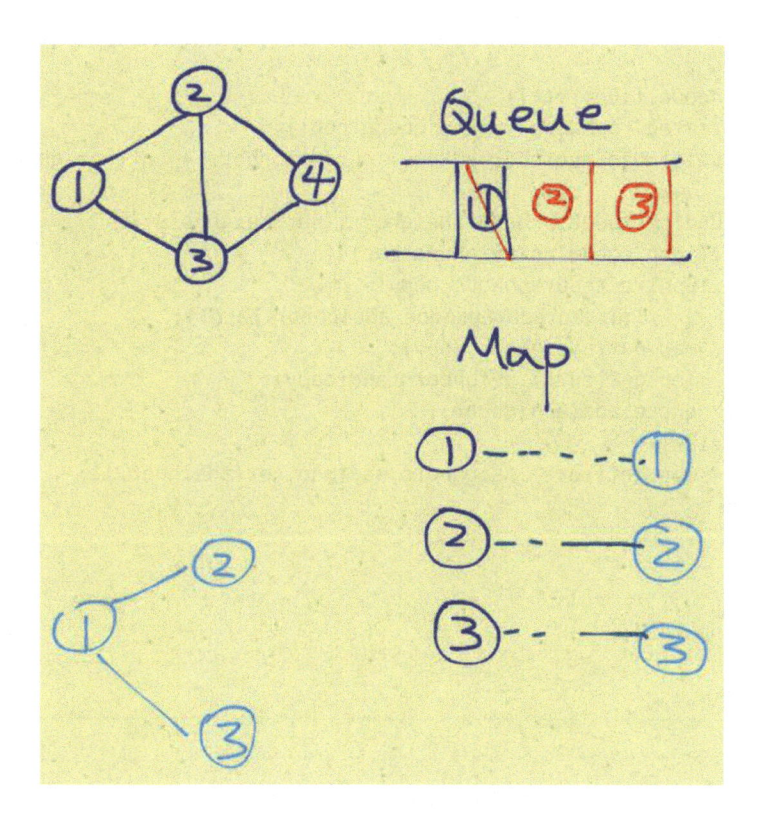

```java
/**
 * Definition for undirected graph.
 * class UndirectedGraphNode {
 *     int label;
 *     ArrayList<UndirectedGraphNode> neighbors;
 *     UndirectedGraphNode(int x) { label = x; neighbors = new
       ArrayList<UndirectedGraphNode>(); }
 * };
 */
public class Solution {
    public UndirectedGraphNode cloneGraph(UndirectedGraphNode node) {
        if(node == null)
            return null;
        
        LinkedList<UndirectedGraphNode> queue = new
            LinkedList<UndirectedGraphNode>();
        HashMap<UndirectedGraphNode, UndirectedGraphNode> map =
                          new
                                HashMap<UndirectedGraphNode,UndirectedGraphNode>();
        
        UndirectedGraphNode newHead = new UndirectedGraphNode(node.label);
        
        queue.add(node);
        map.put(node, newHead);
```

177

```
        while(!queue.isEmpty()){
            UndirectedGraphNode curr = queue.pop();
            ArrayList<UndirectedGraphNode> currNeighbors = curr.neighbors;

            for(UndirectedGraphNode aNeighbor: currNeighbors){
                if(!map.containsKey(aNeighbor)){
                    UndirectedGraphNode copy = new
                        UndirectedGraphNode(aNeighbor.label);
                    map.put(aNeighbor,copy);
                    map.get(curr).neighbors.add(copy);
                    queue.add(aNeighbor);
                }else{
                    map.get(curr).neighbors.add(map.get(aNeighbor));
                }
            }

        }
        return newHead;
    }
}
```

109 Course Schedule

There are a total of n courses you have to take, labeled from 0 to n - 1. Some courses may have prerequisites, for example to take course 0 you have to first take course 1, which is expressed as a pair: [0,1]. Given the total number of courses and a list of prerequisite pairs, is it possible for you to finish all courses?

For example, given 2 and [[1,0]], there are a total of 2 courses to take. To take course 1 you should have finished course 0. So it is possible.

For another example, given 2 and [[1,0],[0,1]], there are a total of 2 courses to take. To take course 1 you should have finished course 0, and to take course 0 you should also have finished course 1. So it is impossible.

109.1 Analysis

This problem can be converted to finding if a graph contains a cycle. The following solution use a breath-first search algorithm. You can read the comment to understand the solution.

109.2 Java Solution 1 - BFS

109 Course Schedule

```java
public boolean canFinish(int numCourses, int[][] prerequisites) {
    if(prerequisites == null){
        throw new IllegalArgumentException("illegal prerequisites array");
    }

    int len = prerequisites.length;

    if(numCourses == 0 || len == 0){
        return true;
    }

    // counter for number of prerequisites
    int[] pCounter = new int[numCourses];
    for(int i=0; i<len; i++){
        pCounter[prerequisites[i][0]]++;
    }

    //store courses that have no prerequisites
    LinkedList<Integer> queue = new LinkedList<Integer>();
    for(int i=0; i<numCourses; i++){
        if(pCounter[i]==0){
            queue.add(i);
        }
    }

    // number of courses that have no prerequisites
    int numNoPre = queue.size();

    while(!queue.isEmpty()){
        int top = queue.remove();
        for(int i=0; i<len; i++){
            // if a course's prerequisite can be satisfied by a course in queue
            if(prerequisites[i][1]==top){
                pCounter[prerequisites[i][0]]--;
                if(pCounter[prerequisites[i][0]]==0){
                    numNoPre++;
                    queue.add(prerequisites[i][0]);
                }
            }
        }
    }

    return numNoPre == numCourses;
}
```

109.3 Java Solution 2 - DFS

109 Course Schedule

```java
public boolean canFinish(int numCourses, int[][] prerequisites) {
    if(prerequisites == null){
        throw new IllegalArgumentException("illegal prerequisites array");
    }

    int len = prerequisites.length;

    if(numCourses == 0 || len == 0){
        return true;
    }

    //track visited courses
    int[] visit = new int[numCourses];

    // use the map to store what courses depend on a course
    HashMap<Integer,ArrayList<Integer>> map = new
        HashMap<Integer,ArrayList<Integer>>();
    for(int[] a: prerequisites){
        if(map.containsKey(a[1])){
            map.get(a[1]).add(a[0]);
        }else{
            ArrayList<Integer> l = new ArrayList<Integer>();
            l.add(a[0]);
            map.put(a[1], l);
        }
    }

    for(int i=0; i<numCourses; i++){
        if(!canFinishDFS(map, visit, i))
            return false;
    }

    return true;
}

private boolean canFinishDFS(HashMap<Integer,ArrayList<Integer>> map, int[]
     visit, int i){
    if(visit[i]==-1)
        return false;
    if(visit[i]==1)
        return true;

    visit[i]=-1;
    if(map.containsKey(i)){
        for(int j: map.get(i)){
            if(!canFinishDFS(map, visit, j))
                return false;
        }
    }
```

```
    visit[i]=1;

    return true;
}
```

Topological Sort Video from Coursera.

110 How Developers Sort in Java?

While analyzing source code of a large number of open source Java projects, I found Java developers frequently sort in two ways. One is using the sort() method of Collections or Arrays, and the other is using sorted data structures, such as TreeMap and TreeSet.

110.1 Using sort() Method

If it is a collection, use Collections.sort() method.

```
// Collections.sort
List<ObjectName> list = new ArrayList<ObjectName>();
Collections.sort(list, new Comparator<ObjectName>() {
  public int compare(ObjectName o1, ObjectName o2) {
    return o1.toString().compareTo(o2.toString());
  }
});
```

If it is an array, use Arrays.sort() method.

```
// Arrays.sort
ObjectName[] arr = new ObjectName[10];
Arrays.sort(arr, new Comparator<ObjectName>() {
  public int compare(ObjectName o1, ObjectName o2) {
    return o1.toString().compareTo(o2.toString());
  }
});
```

This is very convenient if a collection or an array is already set up.

110.2 Using Sorted Data Structures

If it is a list or set, use TreeSet to sort.

```java
// TreeSet
Set<ObjectName> sortedSet = new TreeSet<ObjectName>(new
    Comparator<ObjectName>() {
  public int compare(ObjectName o1, ObjectName o2) {
    return o1.toString().compareTo(o2.toString());
  }
});
sortedSet.addAll(unsortedSet);
```

If it is a map, use TreeMap to sort. TreeMap is sorted by key.

```java
// TreeMap - using String.CASE_INSENSITIVE_ORDER which is a Comparator that
    orders Strings by compareToIgnoreCase
Map<String, Integer> sortedMap = new TreeMap<String,
    Integer>(String.CASE_INSENSITIVE_ORDER);
sortedMap.putAll(unsortedMap);
```

```java
//TreeMap - In general, defined comparator
Map<ObjectName, String> sortedMap = new TreeMap<ObjectName, String>(new
    Comparator<ObjectName>() {
  public int compare(ObjectName o1, ObjectName o2) {
    return o1.toString().compareTo(o2.toString());
  }
});
sortedMap.putAll(unsortedMap);
```

This approach is very useful, if you would do a lot of search operations for the collection. The sorted data structure will give time complexity of O(logn), which is lower than O(n).

110.3 Bad Practices

There are still bad practices, such as using self-defined sorting algorithm. Take the code below for example, not only the algorithm is not efficient, but also it is not readable. This happens a lot in different forms of variations.

```java
double t;
for (int i = 0; i < 2; i++)
  for (int j = i + 1; j < 3; j++)
    if (r[j] < r[i]) {
      t = r[i];
      r[i] = r[j];
      r[j] = t;
    }
```

111 Solution Merge Sort LinkedList in Java

LeetCode - Sort List:
Sort a linked list in O(n log n) time using constant space complexity.

111.1 Keys for solving the problem

- Break the list to two in the middle
- Recursively sort the two sub lists
- Merge the two sub lists

This is my accepted answer for the problem.

```java
package algorithm.sort;

class ListNode {
  int val;
  ListNode next;

  ListNode(int x) {
    val = x;
    next = null;
  }
}

public class SortLinkedList {

  // merge sort
  public static ListNode mergeSortList(ListNode head) {

    if (head == null || head.next == null)
      return head;

    // count total number of elements
    int count = 0;
    ListNode p = head;
    while (p != null) {
      count++;
      p = p.next;
    }
```

111 Solution Merge Sort LinkedList in Java

```java
    // break up to two list
    int middle = count / 2;

    ListNode l = head, r = null;
    ListNode p2 = head;
    int countHalf = 0;
    while (p2 != null) {
      countHalf++;
      ListNode next = p2.next;

      if (countHalf == middle) {
        p2.next = null;
        r = next;
      }
      p2 = next;
    }

    // now we have two parts l and r, recursively sort them
    ListNode h1 = mergeSortList(l);
    ListNode h2 = mergeSortList(r);

    // merge together
    ListNode merged = merge(h1, h2);

    return merged;
  }

  public static ListNode merge(ListNode l, ListNode r) {
    ListNode p1 = l;
    ListNode p2 = r;

    ListNode fakeHead = new ListNode(100);
    ListNode pNew = fakeHead;

    while (p1 != null || p2 != null) {

      if (p1 == null) {
        pNew.next = new ListNode(p2.val);
        p2 = p2.next;
        pNew = pNew.next;
      } else if (p2 == null) {
        pNew.next = new ListNode(p1.val);
        p1 = p1.next;
        pNew = pNew.next;
      } else {
        if (p1.val < p2.val) {
          // if(fakeHead)
          pNew.next = new ListNode(p1.val);
          p1 = p1.next;
          pNew = pNew.next;
```

111 Solution Merge Sort LinkedList in Java

```java
            } else if (p1.val == p2.val) {
                pNew.next = new ListNode(p1.val);
                pNew.next.next = new ListNode(p1.val);
                pNew = pNew.next.next;
                p1 = p1.next;
                p2 = p2.next;

            } else {
                pNew.next = new ListNode(p2.val);
                p2 = p2.next;
                pNew = pNew.next;
            }
        }
    }

    // printList(fakeHead.next);
    return fakeHead.next;
}

public static void main(String[] args) {
    ListNode n1 = new ListNode(2);
    ListNode n2 = new ListNode(3);
    ListNode n3 = new ListNode(4);

    ListNode n4 = new ListNode(3);
    ListNode n5 = new ListNode(4);
    ListNode n6 = new ListNode(5);

    n1.next = n2;
    n2.next = n3;
    n3.next = n4;
    n4.next = n5;
    n5.next = n6;

    n1 = mergeSortList(n1);

    printList(n1);
}

public static void printList(ListNode x) {
    if(x != null){
        System.out.print(x.val + " ");
        while (x.next != null) {
            System.out.print(x.next.val + " ");
            x = x.next;
        }
        System.out.println();
    }

}
```

}

Output:

2 3 3 4 4 5

112 Quicksort Array in Java

Quicksort is a divide and conquer algorithm. It first divides a large list into two smaller sub-lists and then recursively sort the two sub-lists. If we want to sort an array without any extra space, quicksort is a good option. On average, time complexity is O(n log(n)).

The basic step of sorting an array are as follows:

- Select a pivot, normally the middle one
- From both ends, swap elements and make all elements on the left less than the pivot and all elements on the right greater than the pivot
- Recursively sort left part and right part

Here is a very good animation of quicksort.

```java
public class QuickSort {
  public static void main(String[] args) {
    int[] x = { 9, 2, 4, 7, 3, 7, 10 };
    System.out.println(Arrays.toString(x));

    int low = 0;
    int high = x.length - 1;

    quickSort(x, low, high);
    System.out.println(Arrays.toString(x));
  }

  public static void quickSort(int[] arr, int low, int high) {
    if (arr == null || arr.length == 0)
      return;

    if (low >= high)
      return;

    // pick the pivot
    int middle = low + (high - low) / 2;
    int pivot = arr[middle];

    // make left < pivot and right > pivot
    int i = low, j = high;
    while (i <= j) {
```

```
    while (arr[i] < pivot) {
      i++;
    }

    while (arr[j] > pivot) {
      j--;
    }

    if (i <= j) {
      int temp = arr[i];
      arr[i] = arr[j];
      arr[j] = temp;
      i++;
      j--;
    }
  }

  // recursively sort two sub parts
  if (low < j)
    quickSort(arr, low, j);

  if (high > i)
    quickSort(arr, i, high);
  }
}
```

Output:

9 2 4 7 3 7 10 2 3 4 7 7 9 10

113 Solution Sort a linked list using insertion sort in Java

Insertion Sort List:

Sort a linked list using insertion sort.

This is my accepted answer for LeetCode problem - Sort a linked list using insertion sort in Java. It is a complete program.

Before coding for that, here is an example of insertion sort from wiki. You can get an idea of what is insertion sort.

113 Solution Sort a linked list using insertion sort in Java

```
3 7 4 9 5 2 6 1
3 7 4 9 5 2 6 1
3 7 4 9 5 2 6 1
3 4 7 9 5 2 6 1
3 4 7 9 5 2 6 1
3 4 5 7 9 2 6 1
2 3 4 5 7 9 6 1
2 3 4 5 6 7 9 1
1 2 3 4 5 6 7 9
```

Code:

```java
package algorithm.sort;

class ListNode {
  int val;
  ListNode next;

  ListNode(int x) {
    val = x;
    next = null;
  }
}

public class SortLinkedList {
  public static ListNode insertionSortList(ListNode head) {

    if (head == null || head.next == null)
      return head;

    ListNode newHead = new ListNode(head.val);
    ListNode pointer = head.next;

    // loop through each element in the list
    while (pointer != null) {
      // insert this element to the new list

      ListNode innerPointer = newHead;
      ListNode next = pointer.next;

      if (pointer.val <= newHead.val) {
        ListNode oldHead = newHead;
        newHead = pointer;
        newHead.next = oldHead;
```

113 Solution Sort a linked list using insertion sort in Java

```java
    } else {
      while (innerPointer.next != null) {

        if (pointer.val > innerPointer.val && pointer.val <=
            innerPointer.next.val) {
          ListNode oldNext = innerPointer.next;
          innerPointer.next = pointer;
          pointer.next = oldNext;
        }

        innerPointer = innerPointer.next;
      }

      if (innerPointer.next == null && pointer.val > innerPointer.val) {
        innerPointer.next = pointer;
        pointer.next = null;
      }
    }

    // finally
    pointer = next;
  }

  return newHead;
}

public static void main(String[] args) {
  ListNode n1 = new ListNode(2);
  ListNode n2 = new ListNode(3);
  ListNode n3 = new ListNode(4);

  ListNode n4 = new ListNode(3);
  ListNode n5 = new ListNode(4);
  ListNode n6 = new ListNode(5);

  n1.next = n2;
  n2.next = n3;
  n3.next = n4;
  n4.next = n5;
  n5.next = n6;

  n1 = insertionSortList(n1);

  printList(n1);

}

public static void printList(ListNode x) {
  if(x != null){
    System.out.print(x.val + " ");
```

```java
    while (x.next != null) {
      System.out.print(x.next.val + " ");
      x = x.next;
    }
    System.out.println();
  }

 }
}
```

Output:

2 3 3 4 4 5

114 Maximum Gap

Given an unsorted array, find the maximum difference between the successive elements in its sorted form.

Try to solve it in linear time/space. Return 0 if the array contains less than 2 elements. You may assume all elements in the array are non-negative integers and fit in the 32-bit signed integer range.

114.1 Analysis

We can use a bucket-sort like algorithm to solve this problem in time of O(n) and space O(n). The basic idea is to project each element of the array to an array of buckets. Each bucket tracks the maximum and minimum elements. Finally, scanning the bucket list, we can get the maximum gap.

The key part is to get the interval:

```
From: interval * (num[i] - min) = 0 and interval * (max -num[i]) = n
interval = num.length / (max - min)
```

See the internal comment for more details.

114.2 Java Solution

```java
class Bucket{
   int low;
   int high;
   public Bucket(){
      low = -1;
      high = -1;
   }
}
```

```java
public int maximumGap(int[] num) {
    if(num == null || num.length < 2){
        return 0;
    }

    int max = num[0];
    int min = num[0];
    for(int i=1; i<num.length; i++){
        max = Math.max(max, num[i]);
        min = Math.min(min, num[i]);
    }

    // initialize an array of buckets
    Bucket[] buckets = new Bucket[num.length+1]; //project to (0 - n)
    for(int i=0; i<buckets.length; i++){
        buckets[i] = new Bucket();
    }

    double interval = (double) num.length / (max - min);
    //distribute every number to a bucket array
    for(int i=0; i<num.length; i++){
        int index = (int) ((num[i] - min) * interval);

        if(buckets[index].low == -1){
            buckets[index].low = num[i];
            buckets[index].high = num[i];
        }else{
            buckets[index].low = Math.min(buckets[index].low, num[i]);
            buckets[index].high = Math.max(buckets[index].high, num[i]);
        }
    }

    //scan buckets to find maximum gap
    int result = 0;
    int prev = buckets[0].high;
    for(int i=1; i<buckets.length; i++){
        if(buckets[i].low != -1){
            result = Math.max(result, buckets[i].low-prev);
            prev = buckets[i].high;
        }

    }

    return result;
}
```

115 Edit Distance in Java

From Wiki:
> *In computer science, edit distance is a way of quantifying how dissimilar two strings (e.g., words) are to one another by counting the minimum number of operations required to transform one string into the other.*

There are three operations permitted on a word: replace, delete, insert. For example, the edit distance between "a" and "b" is 1, the edit distance between "abc" and "def" is 3. This post analyzes how to calculate edit distance by using dynamic programming.

115.1 Key Analysis

Let dp[i][j] stands for the edit distance between two strings with length i and j, i.e., word1[0,...,i-1] and word2[0,...,j-1]. There is a relation between dp[i][j] and dp[i-1][j-1]. Let's say we transform from one string to another. The first string has length i and it's last character is "x"; the second string has length j and its last character is "y". The following diagram shows the relation.

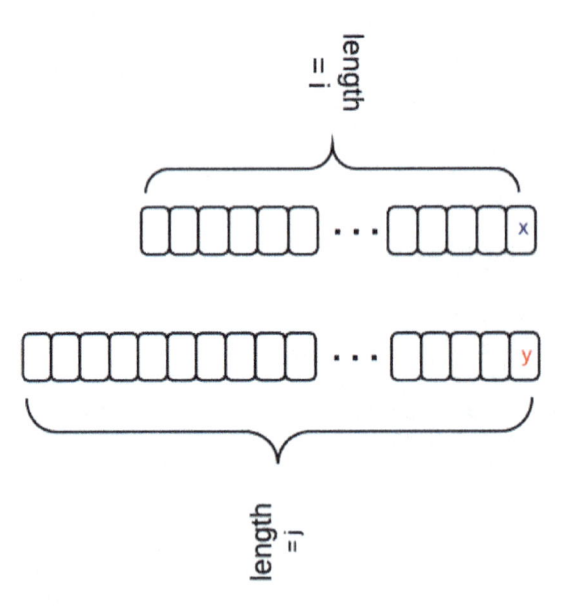

- if x == y, then dp[i][j] == dp[i-1][j-1]
- if x != y, and we insert y for word1, then dp[i][j] = dp[i][j-1] + 1

- if x != y, and we delete x for word1, then dp[i][j] = dp[i-1][j] + 1
- if x != y, and we replace x with y for word1, then dp[i][j] = dp[i-1][j-1] + 1
- When x!=y, dp[i][j] is the min of the three situations.

Initial condition: dp[i][0] = i, dp[0][j] = j

115.2 Java Code

After the analysis above, the code is just a representation of it.

```java
public static int minDistance(String word1, String word2) {
  int len1 = word1.length();
  int len2 = word2.length();

  // len1+1, len2+1, because finally return dp[len1][len2]
  int[][] dp = new int[len1 + 1][len2 + 1];

  for (int i = 0; i <= len1; i++) {
    dp[i][0] = i;
  }

  for (int j = 0; j <= len2; j++) {
    dp[0][j] = j;
  }

  //iterate though, and check last char
  for (int i = 0; i < len1; i++) {
    char c1 = word1.charAt(i);
    for (int j = 0; j < len2; j++) {
      char c2 = word2.charAt(j);

      //if last two chars equal
      if (c1 == c2) {
        //update dp value for +1 length
        dp[i + 1][j + 1] = dp[i][j];
      } else {
        int replace = dp[i][j] + 1;
        int insert = dp[i][j + 1] + 1;
        int delete = dp[i + 1][j] + 1;

        int min = replace > insert ? insert : replace;
        min = delete > min ? min : delete;
        dp[i + 1][j + 1] = min;
      }
    }
  }

  return dp[len1][len2];
}
```

116 Longest Palindromic Substring

Finding the longest palindromic substring is a classic problem of coding interview. This post summarizes 3 different solutions for this problem.

116.1 Naive Approach

Naively, we can simply examine every substring and check if it is palindromic. The time complexity is $O(n^3)$. If this is submitted to LeetCode onlinejudge, an error message will be returned - "Time Limit Exceeded". Therefore, this approach is just a start, we need a better algorithm.

```java
public static String longestPalindrome1(String s) {

	int maxPalinLength = 0;
	String longestPalindrome = null;
	int length = s.length();

	// check all possible sub strings
	for (int i = 0; i < length; i++) {
		for (int j = i + 1; j < length; j++) {
			int len = j - i;
			String curr = s.substring(i, j + 1);
			if (isPalindrome(curr)) {
				if (len > maxPalinLength) {
					longestPalindrome = curr;
					maxPalinLength = len;
				}
			}
		}
	}

	return longestPalindrome;
}

public static boolean isPalindrome(String s) {

	for (int i = 0; i < s.length() - 1; i++) {
		if (s.charAt(i) != s.charAt(s.length() - 1 - i)) {
			return false;
		}
	}
```

```java
    return true;
}
```

116.2 Dynamic Programming

Let s be the input string, i and j are two indices of the string. Define a 2-dimension array "table" and let table[i][j] denote whether a substring from i to j is palindrome.

Start condition:

```
table[i][i] == 1;
table[i][i+1] == 1 => s.charAt(i) == s.charAt(i+1)
```

Changing condition:

```
table[i+1][j-1] == 1 && s.charAt(i) == s.charAt(j)
=>
table[i][j] == 1
```

Time $O(n^2)$ Space $O(n^2)$

```java
public static String longestPalindrome2(String s) {
  if (s == null)
    return null;

  if(s.length() <=1)
    return s;

  int maxLen = 0;
  String longestStr = null;

  int length = s.length();

  int[][] table = new int[length][length];

  //every single letter is palindrome
  for (int i = 0; i < length; i++) {
    table[i][i] = 1;
  }
  printTable(table);

  //e.g. bcba
  //two consecutive same letters are palindrome
  for (int i = 0; i <= length - 2; i++) {
    if (s.charAt(i) == s.charAt(i + 1)){
      table[i][i + 1] = 1;
      longestStr = s.substring(i, i + 2);
    }
  }
```

116 Longest Palindromic Substring

```java
    printTable(table);
    //condition for calculate whole table
    for (int l = 3; l <= length; l++) {
      for (int i = 0; i <= length-l; i++) {
        int j = i + l - 1;
        if (s.charAt(i) == s.charAt(j)) {
          table[i][j] = table[i + 1][j - 1];
          if (table[i][j] == 1 && l > maxLen)
            longestStr = s.substring(i, j + 1);
        } else {
          table[i][j] = 0;
        }
        printTable(table);
      }
    }

    return longestStr;
}
public static void printTable(int[][] x){
  for(int [] y : x){
    for(int z: y){
      System.out.print(z + " ");
    }
    System.out.println();
  }
  System.out.println("------");
}
```

Given a string, we can use the printTable() method to examine the table after execution. For example, if the input string is "dabcba", the final matrix would be the following:

```
1 0 0 0 0 0
0 1 0 0 0 1
0 0 1 0 1 0
0 0 0 1 0 0
0 0 0 0 1 0
0 0 0 0 0 1
```

From the table, we can clearly see that the longest string is in cell table[1][5].

116.3 A Simple Algorithm

Time $O(n^2)$, Space $O(1)$

```java
public String longestPalindrome(String s) {
  if (s.isEmpty()) {
    return null;
  }
```

```java
    if (s.length() == 1) {
      return s;
    }

    String longest = s.substring(0, 1);
    for (int i = 0; i < s.length(); i++) {
      // get longest palindrome with center of i
      String tmp = helper(s, i, i);
      if (tmp.length() > longest.length()) {
        longest = tmp;
      }

      // get longest palindrome with center of i, i+1
      tmp = helper(s, i, i + 1);
      if (tmp.length() > longest.length()) {
        longest = tmp;
      }
    }

    return longest;
  }

  // Given a center, either one letter or two letter,
  // Find longest palindrome
  public String helper(String s, int begin, int end) {
    while (begin >= 0 && end <= s.length() - 1 && s.charAt(begin) ==
        s.charAt(end)) {
      begin--;
      end++;
    }
    return s.substring(begin + 1, end);
  }
```

116.4 Manacher's Algorithm

Manacher's algorithm is much more complicated to figure out, even though it will bring benefit of time complexity of O(n). Since it is not typical, there is no need to waste time on that.

117 Word Break

Given a string s and a dictionary of words dict, determine if s can be segmented into a space-separated sequence of one or more dictionary words. For example, given s = "leetcode", dict = ["leet", "code"]. Return true because "leetcode" can be segmented as "leet code".

117.1 Naive Approach

This problem can be solve by using a naive approach, which is trivial. A discussion can always start from that though.

```java
public class Solution {
    public boolean wordBreak(String s, Set<String> dict) {
          return wordBreakHelper(s, dict, 0);
    }

    public boolean wordBreakHelper(String s, Set<String> dict, int start){
       if(start == s.length())
          return true;

       for(String a: dict){
          int len = a.length();
          int end = start+len;

          //end index should be <= string length
          if(end > s.length())
             continue;

          if(s.substring(start, start+len).equals(a))
             if(wordBreakHelper(s, dict, start+len))
                return true;
       }

       return false;
    }
}
```

Time is O(n²) and exceeds the time limit.

117.2 Dynamic Programming

The key to solve this problem by using dynamic programming approach:

- Define an array t[] such that t[i]==true =>0-(i-1) can be segmented using dictionary
- Initial state t[0] == true

```java
public class Solution {
   public boolean wordBreak(String s, Set<String> dict) {
      boolean[] t = new boolean[s.length()+1];
      t[0] = true; //set first to be true, why?
      //Because we need initial state

      for(int i=0; i<s.length(); i++){
         //should continue from match position
         if(!t[i])
            continue;

         for(String a: dict){
            int len = a.length();
            int end = i + len;
            if(end > s.length())
               continue;

            if(t[end]) continue;

            if(s.substring(i, end).equals(a)){
               t[end] = true;
            }
         }
      }

      return t[s.length()];
   }
}
```

Time: O(string length * dict size)

One tricky part of this solution is the case:

INPUT: "programcreek", ["programcree","program","creek"].

We should get all possible matches, not stop at "programcree".

117.3 Regular Expression

The problem is equivalent to matching the regular expression (leet|code)*, which means that it can be solved by building a DFA in $O(2^{\hat{m}})$ and executing it in $O(n)$. (Thanks to hdante.) Leetcode online judge does not allow using the Pattern class though.

```java
public static void main(String[] args) {
  HashSet<String> dict = new HashSet<String>();
  dict.add("go");
  dict.add("goal");
  dict.add("goals");
  dict.add("special");

  StringBuilder sb = new StringBuilder();

  for(String s: dict){
    sb.append(s + "|");
  }

  String pattern = sb.toString().substring(0, sb.length()-1);
  pattern = "("+pattern+")*";
  Pattern p = Pattern.compile(pattern);
  Matcher m = p.matcher("goalspecial");

  if(m.matches()){
    System.out.println("match");
  }
}
```

117.4 The More Interesting Problem

The dynamic solution can tell us whether the string can be broken to words, but can not tell us what words the string is broken to. So how to get those words?

Check out Word Break II.

118 Word Break II

Given a string s and a dictionary of words dict, add spaces in s to construct a sentence where each word is a valid dictionary word. Return all such possible sentences. For example, given s = "catsanddog", dict = ["cat", "cats", "and", "sand", "dog"], the solution is ["cats and dog", "cat sand dog"].

118.1 Java Solution - Dynamic Programming

This problem is very similar to Word Break. Instead of using a boolean array to track the matched positions, we need to track the actual matched words. Then we can use depth first search to get all the possible paths, i.e., the list of strings.

The following diagram shows the structure of the tracking array.

	Index	Words
c	0	
a	1	
t	2	
s	3	cat
a	4	cats
n	5	
d	6	
d	7	and, sand
o	8	
g	9	
	10	dog

```java
public static List<String> wordBreak(String s, Set<String> dict) {
    //create an array of ArrayList<String>
    List<String> dp[] = new ArrayList[s.length()+1];
    dp[0] = new ArrayList<String>();

    for(int i=0; i<s.length(); i++){
        if( dp[i] == null )
            continue;

        for(String word:dict){
            int len = word.length();
            int end = i+len;
            if(end > s.length())
                continue;

            if(s.substring(i,end).equals(word)){
                if(dp[end] == null){
                    dp[end] = new ArrayList<String>();
                }
                dp[end].add(word);
            }
```

```java
            }
        }
    }

    List<String> result = new LinkedList<String>();
    if(dp[s.length()] == null)
        return result;

    ArrayList<String> temp = new ArrayList<String>();
    dfs(dp, s.length(), result, temp);

    return result;
}

public static void dfs(List<String> dp[],int end,List<String> result,
    ArrayList<String> tmp){
    if(end <= 0){
        String path = tmp.get(tmp.size()-1);
        for(int i=tmp.size()-2; i>=0; i--){
            path += " " + tmp.get(i) ;
        }

        result.add(path);
        return;
    }

    for(String str : dp[end]){
        tmp.add(str);
        dfs(dp, end-str.length(), result, tmp);
        tmp.remove(tmp.size()-1);
    }
}
```

This problem is also useful for solving real problems. Assuming you want to analyze the domain names of the top 10k websites. We can use this solution to break the main part of the domain into words and then get a sense of what kinds of websites are popular. I did this a long time ago and found some interesting results. For example, the most frequent words include "news", "tube", "porn", "etc".

119 Maximum Subarray

Find the contiguous subarray within an array (containing at least one number) which has the largest sum.

For example, given the array $[-2,1,-3,4,-1,2,1,-5,4]$, the contiguous subarray $[4,-1,2,1]$ has the largest sum = 6.

119.1 Wrong Solution

This is a wrong solution, check out the discussion below to see why it is wrong. I put it here just for fun.

```java
public class Solution {
  public int maxSubArray(int[] A) {
    int sum = 0;
    int maxSum = Integer.MIN_VALUE;

    for (int i = 0; i < A.length; i++) {
      sum += A[i];
      maxSum = Math.max(maxSum, sum);

      if (sum < 0)
        sum = 0;
    }

    return maxSum;
  }
}
```

119.2 Dynamic Programming Solution

The changing condition for dynamic programming is "We should ignore the sum of the previous n-1 elements if nth element is greater than the sum."

```java
public class Solution {
  public int maxSubArray(int[] A) {
    int max = A[0];
    int[] sum = new int[A.length];
    sum[0] = A[0];

    for (int i = 1; i < A.length; i++) {
      sum[i] = Math.max(A[i], sum[i - 1] + A[i]);
      max = Math.max(max, sum[i]);
    }

    return max;
  }
}
```

119.3 Simple Solution

Mehdi provided the following solution in his comment.

```java
public int maxSubArray(int[] A) {
    int newsum=A[0];
    int max=A[0];
    for(int i=1;i<A.length;i++){
        newsum=Math.max(newsum+A[i],A[i]);
        max= Math.max(max, newsum);
    }
    return max;
}
```

This problem is asked by Palantir.

120 Maximum Product Subarray

Find the contiguous subarray within an array (containing at least one number) which has the largest product.

For example, given the array [2,3,-2,4], the contiguous subarray [2,3] has the largest product = 6.

120.1 Java Solution 1 - Brute-force

```java
public int maxProduct(int[] A) {
   int max = Integer.MIN_VALUE;

   for(int i=0; i<A.length; i++){
      for(int l=0; l<A.length; l++){
         if(i+l < A.length){
            int product = calProduct(A, i, l);
            max = Math.max(product, max);
         }

      }

   }
   return max;
}

public int calProduct(int[] A, int i, int j){
   int result = 1;
   for(int m=i; m<=j; m++){
      result = result * A[m];
   }
   return result;
}
```

The time of the solution is $O(n^3)$.

120.2 Java Solution 2 - Dynamic Programming

This is similar to maximum subarray. Instead of sum, the sign of number affect the product value.

When iterating the array, each element has two possibilities: positive number or negative number. We need to track a minimum value, so that when a negative number is given, it can also find the maximum value. We define two local variables, one tracks the maximum and the other tracks the minimum.

```java
public int maxProduct(int[] A) {
   if(A==null || A.length==0)
      return 0;

   int maxLocal = A[0];
   int minLocal = A[0];
   int global = A[0];

   for(int i=1; i<A.length; i++){
      int temp = maxLocal;
      maxLocal = Math.max(Math.max(A[i]*maxLocal, A[i]), A[i]*minLocal);
```

```
      minLocal = Math.min(Math.min(A[i]*temp, A[i]), A[i]*minLocal);
      global = Math.max(global, maxLocal);
   }
   return global;
}
```

Time is O(n).

121 Palindrome Partitioning

121.1 Problem

Given a string s, partition s such that every substring of the partition is a palindrome.

Return all possible palindrome partitioning of s.
For example, given s = "aab", Return

```
[
  ["aa","b"],
  ["a","a","b"]
]
```

121.2 Depth-first Search

```java
public ArrayList<ArrayList<String>> partition(String s) {
  ArrayList<ArrayList<String>> result = new ArrayList<ArrayList<String>>();

  if (s == null || s.length() == 0) {
    return result;
  }

  ArrayList<String> partition = new ArrayList<String>();//track each possible
      partition
  addPalindrome(s, 0, partition, result);

  return result;
}

private void addPalindrome(String s, int start, ArrayList<String> partition,
    ArrayList<ArrayList<String>> result) {
  //stop condition
  if (start == s.length()) {
    ArrayList<String> temp = new ArrayList<String>(partition);
    result.add(temp);
    return;
```

```
    }

    for (int i = start + 1; i <= s.length(); i++) {
      String str = s.substring(start, i);
      if (isPalindrome(str)) {
        partition.add(str);
        addPalindrome(s, i, partition, result);
        partition.remove(partition.size() - 1);
      }
    }
  }

  private boolean isPalindrome(String str) {
    int left = 0;
    int right = str.length() - 1;

    while (left < right) {
      if (str.charAt(left) != str.charAt(right)) {
        return false;
      }

      left++;
      right--;
    }

    return true;
  }
```

121.3 Dynamic Programming

The dynamic programming approach is very similar to the problem of longest palindrome substring.

```
public static List<String> palindromePartitioning(String s) {

  List<String> result = new ArrayList<String>();

  if (s == null)
    return result;

  if (s.length() <= 1) {
    result.add(s);
    return result;
  }

  int length = s.length();

  int[][] table = new int[length][length];
```

```java
// l is length, i is index of left boundary, j is index of right boundary
for (int l = 1; l <= length; l++) {
    for (int i = 0; i <= length - l; i++) {
        int j = i + l - 1;
        if (s.charAt(i) == s.charAt(j)) {
            if (l == 1 || l == 2) {
                table[i][j] = 1;
            } else {
                table[i][j] = table[i + 1][j - 1];
            }
            if (table[i][j] == 1) {
                result.add(s.substring(i, j + 1));
            }
        } else {
            table[i][j] = 0;
        }
    }
}

return result;
}
```

122 Palindrome Partitioning II

Given a string s, partition s such that every substring of the partition is a palindrome. Return the minimum cuts needed for a palindrome partitioning of s. For example, given s = "aab", return 1 since the palindrome partitioning ["aa","b"] could be produced using 1 cut.

122.1 Analysis

This problem is similar to Palindrome Partitioning. It can be efficiently solved by using dynamic programming. Unlike "Palindrome Partitioning", we need to maintain two cache arrays, one tracks the partition position and one tracks the number of minimum cut.

122.2 Java Solution

```java
public int minCut(String s) {
    int n = s.length();
```

```java
    boolean dp[][] = new boolean[n][n];
    int cut[] = new int[n];

    for (int j = 0; j < n; j++) {
      cut[j] = j; //set maximum # of cut
      for (int i = 0; i <= j; i++) {
        if (s.charAt(i) == s.charAt(j) && (j - i <= 1 || dp[i+1][j-1])) {
          dp[i][j] = true;

          // if need to cut, add 1 to the previous cut[i-1]
          if (i > 0){
            cut[j] = Math.min(cut[j], cut[i-1] + 1);
          }else{
          // if [0...j] is palindrome, no need to cut
            cut[j] = 0;
          }
        }
      }
    }

    return cut[n-1];
}
```

123 Candy

123.1 Problem

There are N children standing in a line. Each child is assigned a rating value. You are giving candies to these children subjected to the following requirements:
1. Each child must have at least one candy. 2. Children with a higher rating get more candies than their neighbors.
What is the minimum candies you must give?

123.2 Java Solution

This problem can be solved in O(n) time.

We can always assign a neighbor with 1 more if the neighbor has higher a rating value. However, to get the minimum total number, we should always start adding 1s in the ascending order. We can solve this problem by scanning the array from both sides. First, scan the array from left to right, and assign values for all the ascending pairs. Then scan from right to left and assign values to descending pairs.

```java
public int candy(int[] ratings) {
    if (ratings == null || ratings.length == 0) {
        return 0;
    }

    int[] candies = new int[ratings.length];
    candies[0] = 1;

    //from let to right
    for (int i = 1; i < ratings.length; i++) {
        if (ratings[i] > ratings[i - 1]) {
            candies[i] = candies[i - 1] + 1;
        } else {
            // if not ascending, assign 1
            candies[i] = 1;
        }
    }

    int result = candies[ratings.length - 1];

    //from right to left
    for (int i = ratings.length - 2; i >= 0; i--) {
        int cur = 1;
        if (ratings[i] > ratings[i + 1]) {
            cur = candies[i + 1] + 1;
        }

        result += Math.max(cur, candies[i]);
        candies[i] = cur;
    }

    return result;
}
```

124 Jump Game

Given an array of non-negative integers, you are initially positioned at the first index of the array. Each element in the array represents your maximum jump length at that position. Determine if you are able to reach the last index. For example: A = [2,3,1,1,4], return true. A = [3,2,1,0,4], return false.

124.1 Java Solution

We can track the maximum length a position can reach. The key to solve this problem is to find: 1) when the position can not reach next step (return false), and 2) when the maximum can reach the end (return true).

```java
public boolean canJump(int[] A) {
    if(A.length <= 1)
        return true;

    int max = A[0];

    for(int i=0; i<A.length; i++){
        //if not enough to go to next
        if(max <= i && A[i] == 0)
            return false;

        //update max
        if(i + A[i] > max){
            max = i + A[i];
        }

        //max is enough to reach the end
        if(max >= A.length-1)
            return true;
    }

    return false;
}
```

125 Best Time to Buy and Sell Stock

Say you have an array for which the ith element is the price of a given stock on day i.

If you were only permitted to complete at most one transaction (ie, buy one and sell one share of the stock), design an algorithm to find the maximum profit.

125.1 Naive Approach

The naive approach exceeds time limit.

```java
public int maxProfit(int[] prices) {
    if(prices == null || prices.length < 2){
        return 0;
    }
```

```java
    int profit = Integer.MIN_VALUE;
    for(int i=0; i<prices.length-1; i++){
        for(int j=0; j< prices.length; j++){
            if(profit < prices[j] - prices[i]){
                profit = prices[j] - prices[i];
            }
        }
    }
    return profit;
}
```

125.2 Efficient Approach

Instead of keeping track of largest element in the array, we track the maximum profit so far.

```java
public int maxProfit(int[] prices) {
    int profit = 0;
    int minElement = Integer.MAX_VALUE;
    for(int i=0; i<prices.length; i++){
        profit = Math.max(profit, prices[i]-minElement);
        minElement = Math.min(minElement, prices[i]);
    }
    return profit;
}
```

126 Best Time to Buy and Sell Stock II

Say you have an array for which the ith element is the price of a given stock on day i.

Design an algorithm to find the maximum profit. You may complete as many transactions as you like (ie, buy one and sell one share of the stock multiple times). However, you may not engage in multiple transactions at the same time (ie, you must sell the stock before you buy again).

126.1 Analysis

This problem can be viewed as finding all ascending sequences. For example, given 5, 1, 2, 3, 4, buy at 1 & sell at 4 is the same as buy at 1 &sell at 2 & buy at 2& sell at 3 & buy at 3 & sell at 4.

We can scan the array once, and find all pairs of elements that are in ascending order.

126.2 Java Solution

```java
public int maxProfit(int[] prices) {
   int profit = 0;
   for(int i=1; i<prices.length; i++){
      int diff = prices[i]-prices[i-1];
      if(diff > 0){
         profit += diff;
      }
   }
   return profit;
}
```

127 Best Time to Buy and Sell Stock III

Say you have an array for which the ith element is the price of a given stock on day i.

Design an algorithm to find the maximum profit. You may complete at most two transactions.

Note: A transaction is a buy & a sell. You may not engage in multiple transactions at the same time (ie, you must sell the stock before you buy again).

127.1 Analysis

Comparing to I and II, III limits the number of transactions to 2. This can be solve by "devide and conquer". We use left[i] to track the maximum profit for transactions before i, and use right[i] to track the maximum profit for transactions after i. You can use the following example to understand the Java solution:

```
Prices: 1 4 5 7 6 3 2 9
left = [0, 3, 4, 6, 6, 6, 6, 8]
right= [8, 7, 7, 7, 7, 7, 7, 0]
```

The maximum profit = 13

127.2 Java Solution

```java
public int maxProfit(int[] prices) {
  if (prices == null || prices.length < 2) {
    return 0;
  }

  //highest profit in 0 ... i
  int[] left = new int[prices.length];
  int[] right = new int[prices.length];

  // DP from left to right
  left[0] = 0;
  int min = prices[0];
  for (int i = 1; i < prices.length; i++) {
    min = Math.min(min, prices[i]);
    left[i] = Math.max(left[i - 1], prices[i] - min);
  }

  // DP from right to left
  right[prices.length - 1] = 0;
  int max = prices[prices.length - 1];
  for (int i = prices.length - 2; i >= 0; i--) {
    max = Math.max(max, prices[i]);
    right[i] = Math.max(right[i + 1], max - prices[i]);
  }

  int profit = 0;
  for (int i = 0; i < prices.length; i++) {
    profit = Math.max(profit, left[i] + right[i]);
  }

  return profit;
}
```

128 Best Time to Buy and Sell Stock IV

128.1 Problem

Say you have an array for which the ith element is the price of a given stock on day i. Design an algorithm to find the maximum profit. You may complete at most k transactions.

Note: You may not engage in multiple transactions at the same time (ie, you must sell the stock before you buy again).

128 Best Time to Buy and Sell Stock IV

128.2 Analysis

This is a generalized version of Best Time to Buy and Sell Stock III. If we can solve this problem, we can also use k=2 to solve III.

The problem can be solve by using dynamic programming. The relation is:

```
local[i][j] = max(global[i-1][j-1] + max(diff,0), local[i-1][j]+diff)
global[i][j] = max(local[i][j], global[i-1][j])
```

We track two arrays - local and global. The local array tracks maximum profit of j transactions & the last transaction is on ith day. The global array tracks the maximum profit of j transactions until ith day.

128.3 Java Solution - 2D Dynamic Programming

```java
public int maxProfit(int k, int[] prices) {
  int len = prices.length;

  if (len < 2 || k <= 0)
    return 0;

  // ignore this line
  if (k == 1000000000)
    return 1648961;

  int[][] local = new int[len][k + 1];
  int[][] global = new int[len][k + 1];

  for (int i = 1; i < len; i++) {
    int diff = prices[i] - prices[i - 1];
    for (int j = 1; j <= k; j++) {
      local[i][j] = Math.max(
          global[i - 1][j - 1] + Math.max(diff, 0),
          local[i - 1][j] + diff);
      global[i][j] = Math.max(global[i - 1][j], local[i][j]);
    }
  }

  return global[prices.length - 1][k];
}
```

128.4 Java Solution - 1D Dynamic Programming

The solution above can be simplified to be the following:

```java
public int maxProfit(int k, int[] prices) {
```

```java
    if (prices.length < 2 || k <= 0)
      return 0;

    //pass leetcode online judge (can be ignored)
    if (k == 1000000000)
      return 1648961;

    int[] local = new int[k + 1];
    int[] global = new int[k + 1];

    for (int i = 0; i < prices.length - 1; i++) {
      int diff = prices[i + 1] - prices[i];
      for (int j = k; j >= 1; j--) {
        local[j] = Math.max(global[j - 1] + Math.max(diff, 0), local[j] + diff);
        global[j] = Math.max(local[j], global[j]);
      }
    }

    return global[k];
}
```

129 Dungeon Game

Example:

```
-2 (K) -3  3
-5  -10  1
10  30  -5 (P)
```

129.1 Java Solution

This problem can be solved by using dynamic programming. We maintain a 2-D table. h[i][j] is the minimum health value before he enters (i,j). h[0][0] is the value of the answer. The left part is filling in numbers to the table.

```java
public int calculateMinimumHP(int[][] dungeon) {
    int m = dungeon.length;
    int n = dungeon[0].length;

    //init dp table
    int[][] h = new int[m][n];

    h[m - 1][n - 1] = Math.max(1 - dungeon[m - 1][n - 1], 1);
```

```java
//init last row
for (int i = m - 2; i >= 0; i--) {
    h[i][n - 1] = Math.max(h[i + 1][n - 1] - dungeon[i][n - 1], 1);
}

//init last column
for (int j = n - 2; j >= 0; j--) {
    h[m - 1][j] = Math.max(h[m - 1][j + 1] - dungeon[m - 1][j], 1);
}

//calculate dp table
for (int i = m - 2; i >= 0; i--) {
    for (int j = n - 2; j >= 0; j--) {
        int down = Math.max(h[i + 1][j] - dungeon[i][j], 1);
        int right = Math.max(h[i][j + 1] - dungeon[i][j], 1);
        h[i][j] = Math.min(right, down);
    }
}

return h[0][0];
}
```

130 House Robber

You are a professional robber planning to rob houses along a street. Each house has a certain amount of money stashed, the only constraint stopping you from robbing each of them is that adjacent houses have security system connected and it will automatically contact the police if two adjacent houses were broken into on the same night.

Given a list of non-negative integers representing the amount of money of each house, determine the maximum amount of money you can rob tonight without alerting the police.

130.1 Java Solution 1 - Dynamic Programming

The key is to find the relation dp[i] = Math.max(dp[i-1], dp[i-2]+num[i-1]).

```java
public int rob(int[] num) {
    if(num==null || num.length==0)
        return 0;

    int n = num.length;

    int[] dp = new int[n+1];
```

```
    dp[0]=0;
    dp[1]=num[0];

    for (int i=2; i<n+1; i++){
       dp[i] = Math.max(dp[i-1], dp[i-2]+num[i-1]);
    }

    return dp[n];
}
```

130.2 Java Solution 2

We can use two variables, even and odd, to track the maximum value so far as iterating the array. You can use the following example to walk through the code.

```
50 1 1 50
```

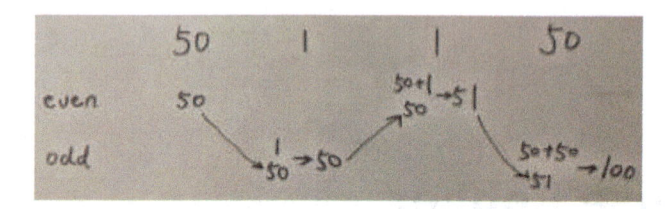

```
public int rob(int[] num) {
   if(num==null || num.length == 0)
      return 0;

   int even = 0;
   int odd = 0;

   for (int i = 0; i < num.length; i++) {
      if (i % 2 == 0) {
         even += num[i];
         even = even > odd ? even : odd;
      } else {
         odd += num[i];
         odd = even > odd ? even : odd;
      }
   }

   return even > odd ? even : odd;
}
```

131 House Robber II

After robbing those houses on that street, the thief has found himself a new place for his thievery so that he will not get too much attention. This time, all houses at this place are arranged in a circle. That means the first house is the neighbor of the last one. Meanwhile, the security system for these houses remain the same as for those in the previous street.

Given a list of non-negative integers representing the amount of money of each house, determine the maximum amount of money you can rob tonight without alerting the police.

131.1 Analysis

This is an extension of House Robber. There are two cases here 1) 1st element is included and last is not included 2) 1st is not included and last is included. Therefore, we can use the similar dynamic programming approach to scan the array twice and get the larger value.

131.2 Java Solution

```java
public int rob(int[] nums) {
    if(nums==null||nums.length==0)
        return 0;

    int n = nums.length;

    if(n==1){
        return nums[0];
    }
    if(n==2){
        return Math.max(nums[1], nums[0]);
    }

    //include 1st element, and not last element
    int[] dp = new int[n+1];
    dp[0]=0;
    dp[1]=nums[0];

    for(int i=2; i<n; i++){
        dp[i] = Math.max(dp[i-1], dp[i-2]+nums[i-1]);
    }
```

```
    //not include frist element, and include last element
    int[] dr = new int[n+1];
    dr[0]=0;
    dr[1]=nums[1];

    for(int i=2; i<n; i++){
      dr[i] = Math.max(dr[i-1], dr[i-2]+nums[i]);
    }

    return Math.max(dp[n-1], dr[n-1]);
}
```

132 Distinct Subsequences Total

Given a string S and a string T, count the number of distinct subsequences of T in S.

A subsequence of a string is a new string which is formed from the original string by deleting some (can be none) of the characters without disturbing the relative positions of the remaining characters. (ie, "ACE" is a subsequence of "ABCDE" while "AEC" is not).

Here is an example: S = "rabbbit", T = "rabbit"

Return 3.

132.1 Thoughts

When you see string problem that is about subsequence or matching, dynamic programming method should come to your mind naturally. The key is to find the changing condition.

132.2 Java Solution 1

Let W(i, j) stand for the number of subsequences of S(0, i) in T(0, j). If S.charAt(i) == T.charAt(j), W(i, j) = W(i-1, j-1) + W(i-1,j); Otherwise, W(i, j) = W(i-1,j).

```java
public int numDistincts(String S, String T) {
  int[][] table = new int[S.length() + 1][T.length() + 1];

  for (int i = 0; i < S.length(); i++)
    table[i][0] = 1;

  for (int i = 1; i <= S.length(); i++) {
    for (int j = 1; j <= T.length(); j++) {
      if (S.charAt(i - 1) == T.charAt(j - 1)) {
        table[i][j] += table[i - 1][j] + table[i - 1][j - 1];
```

```
    } else {
      table[i][j] += table[i - 1][j];
    }
   }
  }

  return table[S.length()][T.length()];
}
```

132.3 Java Solution 2

Do NOT write something like this, even it can also pass the online judge.

```
public int numDistinct(String S, String T) {
  HashMap<Character, ArrayList<Integer>> map = new HashMap<Character,
      ArrayList<Integer>>();

  for (int i = 0; i < T.length(); i++) {
    if (map.containsKey(T.charAt(i))) {
      map.get(T.charAt(i)).add(i);
    } else {
      ArrayList<Integer> temp = new ArrayList<Integer>();
      temp.add(i);
      map.put(T.charAt(i), temp);
    }
  }

  int[] result = new int[T.length() + 1];
  result[0] = 1;

  for (int i = 0; i < S.length(); i++) {
    char c = S.charAt(i);

    if (map.containsKey(c)) {
      ArrayList<Integer> temp = map.get(c);
      int[] old = new int[temp.size()];

      for (int j = 0; j < temp.size(); j++)
        old[j] = result[temp.get(j)];

      // the relation
      for (int j = 0; j < temp.size(); j++)
        result[temp.get(j) + 1] = result[temp.get(j) + 1] + old[j];
    }
  }

  return result[T.length()];
}
```

133 Single Number

The problem:
> Given an array of integers, every element appears twice except for one. Find that single one.

133.1 Thoughts

The key to solve this problem is bit manipulation. XOR will return 1 only on two different bits. So if two numbers are the same, XOR will return 0. Finally only one number left.

133.2 Java Solution

```java
public class Solution {
   public int singleNumber(int[] A) {
      int x=0;

      for(int a: A){
         x = x ^ a;
      }

      return x;
   }
}
```

The question now is do you know any other ways to do this?

134 Single Number II

134.1 Problem

Given an array of integers, every element appears three times except for one. Find that single one.

134.2 Java Solution

This problem is similar to Single Number.

```java
public int singleNumber(int[] A) {
    int ones = 0, twos = 0, threes = 0;
    for (int i = 0; i < A.length; i++) {
        twos |= ones & A[i];
        ones ^= A[i];
        threes = ones & twos;
        ones &= ~threes;
        twos &= ~threes;
    }
    return ones;
}
```

135 Twitter Codility Problem Max Binary Gap

Problem: Get maximum binary Gap.
For example, 9's binary form is 1001, the gap is 2.

135.1 Thoughts

The key to solve this problem is the fact that an integer x & 1 will get the last digit of the integer.

135.2 Java Solution

```java
public class Solution {
    public static int solution(int N) {
        int max = 0;
        int count = -1;
        int r = 0;

        while (N > 0) {
            // get right most bit & shift right
            r = N & 1;
            N = N >> 1;

            if (0 == r && count >= 0) {
                count++;
```

```
      }

      if (1 == r) {
        max = count > max ? count : max;
        count = 0;
      }
    }

    return max;
  }

  public static void main(String[] args) {
    System.out.println(solution(9));
  }
}
```

136 Number of 1 Bits

136.1 Problem

Write a function that takes an unsigned integer and returns the number of '1' bits it has (also known as the Hamming weight).

For example, the 32-bit integer '11' has binary representation 00000000000000000000000000001011, so the function should return 3.

136.2 Java Solution

```java
public int hammingWeight(int n) {
   int count = 0;
   for(int i=1; i<33; i++){
      if(getBit(n, i) == true){
         count++;
      }
   }
   return count;
}

public boolean getBit(int n, int i){
   return (n & (1 << i)) != 0;
}
```

137 Reverse Bits

137.1 Problem

Reverse bits of a given 32 bits unsigned integer.

For example, given input 43261596 (represented in binary as 00000010100101000001111010011100), return 964176192 (represented in binary as 00111001011110000010100101000000).

Follow up: If this function is called many times, how would you optimize it?

Related problem: Reverse Integer

137.2 Java Solution

```java
public int reverseBits(int n) {
  for (int i = 0; i < 16; i++) {
    n = swapBits(n, i, 32 - i - 1);
  }

  return n;
}

public int swapBits(int n, int i, int j) {
  int a = (n >> i) & 1;
  int b = (n >> j) & 1;

  if ((a ^ b) != 0) {
    return n ^= (1 << i) | (1 << j);
  }

  return n;
}
```

138 Repeated DNA Sequences

138 Repeated DNA Sequences

138.1 Problem

All DNA is composed of a series of nucleotides abbreviated as A, C, G, and T, for example: "ACGAATTCCG". When studying DNA, it is sometimes useful to identify repeated sequences within the DNA.

Write a function to find all the 10-letter-long sequences (substrings) that occur more than once in a DNA molecule.

For example, given s = "AAAAACCCCCAAAAACCCCCAAAAAGGGTTT", return: ["AAAAACCCCC", "CCCCCAAAAA"].

138.2 Java Solution

The key to solve this problem is that each of the 4 nucleotides can be stored in 2 bits. So the 10-letter-long sequence can be converted to 20-bits-long integer. The following is a Java solution. You may use an example to manually execute the program and see how it works.

```java
public List<String> findRepeatedDnaSequences(String s) {
  List<String> result = new ArrayList<String>();

  int len = s.length();
  if (len < 10) {
    return result;
  }

  Map<Character, Integer> map = new HashMap<Character, Integer>();
  map.put('A', 0);
  map.put('C', 1);
  map.put('G', 2);
  map.put('T', 3);

  Set<Integer> temp = new HashSet<Integer>();
  Set<Integer> added = new HashSet<Integer>();

  int hash = 0;
  for (int i = 0; i < len; i++) {
    if (i < 9) {
      //each ACGT fit 2 bits, so left shift 2
      hash = (hash << 2) + map.get(s.charAt(i));
    } else {
      hash = (hash << 2) + map.get(s.charAt(i));
      //make length of hash to be 20
      hash = hash & (1 << 20) - 1;

      if (temp.contains(hash) && !added.contains(hash)) {
        result.add(s.substring(i - 9, i + 1));
        added.add(hash); //track added
      } else {
```

```
        temp.add(hash);
      }
    }

  }

  return result;
}
```

139 Bitwise AND of Numbers Range

Given a range [m, n] where 0 <= m <= n <= 2147483647, return the bitwise AND of all numbers in this range, inclusive. For example, given the range [5, 7], you should return 4.

139.1 Java Solution

The key to solve this problem is bitwise AND consecutive numbers. You can use the following example to walk through the code.

```
8 4 2 1
---------------
5 | 0 1 0 1
6 | 0 1 1 0
7 | 0 1 1 1
```

```java
public int rangeBitwiseAnd(int m, int n) {
    while (n > m) {
        n = n & n - 1;
    }
    return m & n;
}
```

140 Permutations

Given a collection of numbers, return all possible permutations.

For example,

140 Permutations

[1,2,3] have the following permutations:
[1,2,3], [1,3,2], [2,1,3], [2,3,1], [3,1,2], and [3,2,1].

140.1 Java Solution 1

We can get all permutations by the following steps:

```
[1]
[2, 1]
[1, 2]
[3, 2, 1]
[2, 3, 1]
[2, 1, 3]
[3, 1, 2]
[1, 3, 2]
[1, 2, 3]
```

Loop through the array, in each iteration, a new number is added to different locations of results of previous iteration. Start from an empty List.

```java
public ArrayList<ArrayList<Integer>> permute(int[] num) {
  ArrayList<ArrayList<Integer>> result = new ArrayList<ArrayList<Integer>>();

  //start from an empty list
  result.add(new ArrayList<Integer>());

  for (int i = 0; i < num.length; i++) {
    //list of list in current iteration of the array num
    ArrayList<ArrayList<Integer>> current = new
       ArrayList<ArrayList<Integer>>();

    for (ArrayList<Integer> l : result) {
      // # of locations to insert is largest index + 1
      for (int j = 0; j < l.size()+1; j++) {
        // + add num[i] to different locations
        l.add(j, num[i]);

        ArrayList<Integer> temp = new ArrayList<Integer>(l);
        current.add(temp);

        //System.out.println(temp);

        // - remove num[i] add
        l.remove(j);
      }
    }

    result = new ArrayList<ArrayList<Integer>>(current);
  }
}
```

```
    return result;
}
```

140.2 Java Solution 2

We can also recursively solve this problem. Swap each element with each element after it.

```java
public ArrayList<ArrayList<Integer>> permute(int[] num) {
    ArrayList<ArrayList<Integer>> result = new ArrayList<ArrayList<Integer>>();
    permute(num, 0, result);
    return result;
}

void permute(int[] num, int start, ArrayList<ArrayList<Integer>> result) {

    if (start >= num.length) {
        ArrayList<Integer> item = convertArrayToList(num);
        result.add(item);
    }

    for (int j = start; j <= num.length - 1; j++) {
        swap(num, start, j);
        permute(num, start + 1, result);
        swap(num, start, j);
    }
}

private ArrayList<Integer> convertArrayToList(int[] num) {
    ArrayList<Integer> item = new ArrayList<Integer>();
    for (int h = 0; h < num.length; h++) {
        item.add(num[h]);
    }
    return item;
}

private void swap(int[] a, int i, int j) {
    int temp = a[i];
    a[i] = a[j];
    a[j] = temp;
}
```

141 Permutations II

Given a collection of numbers that might contain duplicates, return all possible unique permutations.

For example, [1,1,2] have the following unique permutations:
[1,1,2], [1,2,1], and [2,1,1].

141.1 Basic Idea

For each number in the array, swap it with every element after it. To avoid duplicate, we need to check the existing sequence first.

141.2 Java Solution 1

```java
public ArrayList<ArrayList<Integer>> permuteUnique(int[] num) {
    ArrayList<ArrayList<Integer>> result = new ArrayList<ArrayList<Integer>>();
    permuteUnique(num, 0, result);
    return result;
}

private void permuteUnique(int[] num, int start,
    ArrayList<ArrayList<Integer>> result) {

    if (start >= num.length ) {
        ArrayList<Integer> item = convertArrayToList(num);
        result.add(item);
    }

    for (int j = start; j <= num.length-1; j++) {
        if (containsDuplicate(num, start, j)) {
            swap(num, start, j);
            permuteUnique(num, start + 1, result);
            swap(num, start, j);
        }
    }
}

private ArrayList<Integer> convertArrayToList(int[] num) {
    ArrayList<Integer> item = new ArrayList<Integer>();
    for (int h = 0; h < num.length; h++) {
        item.add(num[h]);
    }
    return item;
}

private boolean containsDuplicate(int[] arr, int start, int end) {
```

```java
    for (int i = start; i <= end-1; i++) {
      if (arr[i] == arr[end]) {
        return false;
      }
    }
    return true;
}

private void swap(int[] a, int i, int j) {
    int temp = a[i];
    a[i] = a[j];
    a[j] = temp;
}
```

141.3 Java Solution 2

Use set to maintain uniqueness:

```java
public static ArrayList<ArrayList<Integer>> permuteUnique(int[] num) {
    ArrayList<ArrayList<Integer>> returnList = new 
       ArrayList<ArrayList<Integer>>();
    returnList.add(new ArrayList<Integer>());

    for (int i = 0; i < num.length; i++) {
      Set<ArrayList<Integer>> currentSet = new HashSet<ArrayList<Integer>>();
      for (List<Integer> l : returnList) {
        for (int j = 0; j < l.size() + 1; j++) {
          l.add(j, num[i]);
          ArrayList<Integer> T = new ArrayList<Integer>(l);
          l.remove(j);
          currentSet.add(T);
        }
      }
      returnList = new ArrayList<ArrayList<Integer>>(currentSet);
    }

    return returnList;
}
```

Thanks to Milan for such a simple solution!

142 Permutation Sequence

The set [1,2,3,...,n] contains a total of n! unique permutations.

142 Permutation Sequence

By listing and labeling all of the permutations in order, We get the following sequence (ie, for n = 3):

"123"
"132"
"213"
"231"
"312"
"321"

Given n and k, return the kth permutation sequence.
Note: Given n will be between 1 and 9 inclusive.

142.1 Thoughts

Naively loop through all cases will not work.

142.2 Java Solution 1

```java
public class Solution {
  public String getPermutation(int n, int k) {

    // initialize all numbers
    ArrayList<Integer> numberList = new ArrayList<Integer>();
    for (int i = 1; i <= n; i++) {
      numberList.add(i);
    }

    // change k to be index
    k--;

    // set factorial of n
    int mod = 1;
    for (int i = 1; i <= n; i++) {
      mod = mod * i;
    }

    String result = "";

    // find sequence
    for (int i = 0; i < n; i++) {
      mod = mod / (n - i);
      // find the right number(curIndex) of
      int curIndex = k / mod;
      // update k
      k = k % mod;
```

```java
      // get number according to curIndex
      result += numberList.get(curIndex);
      // remove from list
      numberList.remove(curIndex);
    }

    return result.toString();
  }
}
```

142.3 Java Solution 2

```java
public class Solution {
  public String getPermutation(int n, int k) {
    boolean[] output = new boolean[n];
    StringBuilder buf = new StringBuilder("");

    int[] res = new int[n];
    res[0] = 1;

    for (int i = 1; i < n; i++)
      res[i] = res[i - 1] * i;

    for (int i = n - 1; i >= 0; i--) {
      int s = 1;

      while (k > res[i]) {
        s++;
        k = k - res[i];
      }

      for (int j = 0; j < n; j++) {
        if (j + 1 <= s && output[j]) {
          s++;
        }
      }

      output[s - 1] = true;
      buf.append(Integer.toString(s));
    }

    return buf.toString();
  }
}
```

143 Generate Parentheses

Given n pairs of parentheses, write a function to generate all combinations of well-formed parentheses.

For example, given n = 3, a solution set is:

```
"((()))", "(()())", "(())()", "()(())", "()()()"
```

143.1 Java Solution

Read the following solution, give n=2, walk though the code. Hopefully you will quickly get an idea.

```java
public List<String> generateParenthesis(int n) {
  ArrayList<String> result = new ArrayList<String>();
  ArrayList<Integer> diff = new ArrayList<Integer>();

  result.add("");
  diff.add(0);

  for (int i = 0; i < 2 * n; i++) {
    ArrayList<String> temp1 = new ArrayList<String>();
    ArrayList<Integer> temp2 = new ArrayList<Integer>();

    for (int j = 0; j < result.size(); j++) {
      String s = result.get(j);
      int k = diff.get(j);

      if (i < 2 * n - 1) {
        temp1.add(s + "(");
        temp2.add(k + 1);
      }

      if (k > 0 && i < 2 * n - 1 || k == 1 && i == 2 * n - 1) {
        temp1.add(s + ")");
        temp2.add(k - 1);
      }
    }

    result = new ArrayList<String>(temp1);
    diff = new ArrayList<Integer>(temp2);
  }

  return result;
}
```

}

Solution is provided first now. I will come back and draw a diagram to explain the solution.

144 Combination Sum

Given a set of candidate numbers (C) and a target number (T), find all unique combinations in C where the candidate numbers sums to T. The same repeated number may be chosen from C unlimited number of times.

Note: All numbers (including target) will be positive integers. Elements in a combination (a1, a2, ... , ak) must be in non-descending order. (ie, a1 <= a2 <= ... <= ak). The solution set must not contain duplicate combinations. For example, given candidate set 2,3,6,7 and target 7, A solution set is:

[7]
[2, 2, 3]

144.1 Thoughts

The first impression of this problem should be depth-first search(DFS). To solve DFS problem, recursion is a normal implementation.

Note that the candidates array is not sorted, we need to sort it first.

144.2 Java Solution

```java
public ArrayList<ArrayList<Integer>> combinationSum(int[] candidates, int target) {
    ArrayList<ArrayList<Integer>> result = new ArrayList<ArrayList<Integer>>();

    if(candidates == null || candidates.length == 0) return result;

    ArrayList<Integer> current = new ArrayList<Integer>();
    Arrays.sort(candidates);

    combinationSum(candidates, target, 0, current, result);

    return result;
}

public void combinationSum(int[] candidates, int target, int j,
    ArrayList<Integer> curr, ArrayList<ArrayList<Integer>> result){
```

```java
    if(target == 0){
        ArrayList<Integer> temp = new ArrayList<Integer>(curr);
        result.add(temp);
        return;
    }

    for(int i=j; i<candidates.length; i++){
        if(target < candidates[i])
            return;

        curr.add(candidates[i]);
        combinationSum(candidates, target - candidates[i], i, curr, result);
        curr.remove(curr.size()-1);
    }
}
```

145 Combination Sum II

Given a collection of candidate numbers (C) and a target number (T), find all unique combinations in C where the candidate numbers sums to T. Each number in C may only be used ONCE in the combination.

Note: 1) All numbers (including target) will be positive integers. 2) Elements in a combination (a1, a2, ... , ak) must be in non-descending order. (ie, a1 $\leq$ a2 $\leq$ ... $\leq$ ak). 3) The solution set must not contain duplicate combinations.

145.1 Java Solution

This problem is an extension of Combination Sum. The difference is one number in the array can only be used ONCE.

```java
public List<ArrayList<Integer>> combinationSum2(int[] num, int target) {
    ArrayList<ArrayList<Integer>> result = new ArrayList<ArrayList<Integer>>();
    if(num == null || num.length == 0)
        return result;

    Arrays.sort(num);

    ArrayList<Integer> temp = new ArrayList<Integer>();
    getCombination(num, 0, target, temp, result);

    HashSet<ArrayList<Integer>> set = new HashSet<ArrayList<Integer>>(result);

    //remove duplicate lists
    result.clear();
```

```java
        result.addAll(set);

    return result;
}

public void getCombination(int[] num, int start, int target,
    ArrayList<Integer> temp, ArrayList<ArrayList<Integer>> result){
    if(target == 0){
        ArrayList<Integer> t = new ArrayList<Integer>(temp);
        result.add(t);
        return;
    }

    for(int i=start; i<num.length; i++){
        if(target < num[i])
            continue;

        temp.add(num[i]);
        getCombination(num, i+1, target-num[i], temp, result);
        temp.remove(temp.size()-1);
    }
}
```

146 Combination Sum III

Find all possible combinations of k numbers that add up to a number n, given that only numbers from 1 to 9 can be used and each combination should be a unique set of numbers.

Ensure that numbers within the set are sorted in ascending order.

Example 1: Input: k = 3, n = 7 Output: [[1,2,4]] Example 2: Input: k = 3, n = 9 Output: [[1,2,6], [1,3,5], [2,3,4]]

146.1 Analysis

Related problems: Combination Sum, Combination Sum II.

146.2 Java Solution

```java
public ArrayList<ArrayList<Integer>> combinationSum3(int k, int n) {
    ArrayList<ArrayList<Integer>> result = new ArrayList<ArrayList<Integer>>();
    ArrayList<Integer> list = new ArrayList<Integer>();
    dfs(result, 1, n, list, k);
```

```java
        return result;
    }

    public void dfs(ArrayList<ArrayList<Integer>> result, int start, int sum,
        ArrayList<Integer> list, int k){
        if(sum==0 && list.size()==k){
            ArrayList<Integer> temp = new ArrayList<Integer>();
            temp.addAll(list);
            result.add(temp);
        }

        for(int i=start; i<=9; i++){
            if(sum-i<0) break;
            if(list.size()>k) break;

            list.add(i);
            dfs(result, i+1, sum-i, list, k);
            list.remove(list.size()-1);
        }
    }
```

147 Combinations

147.1 Problem

Given two integers n and k, return all possible combinations of k numbers out of 1 ... n.

For example, if n = 4 and k = 2, a solution is:

```
[
  [2,4],
  [3,4],
  [2,3],
  [1,2],
  [1,3],
  [1,4],
]
```

147.2 Java Solution 1 (Recursion)

This is my naive solution. It passed the online judge. I first initialize a list with only one element, and then recursively add available elements to it.

147 Combinations

```java
public ArrayList<ArrayList<Integer>> combine(int n, int k) {
  ArrayList<ArrayList<Integer>> result = new ArrayList<ArrayList<Integer>>();

  //illegal case
  if (k > n) {
    return null;
  //if k==n
  } else if (k == n) {
    ArrayList<Integer> temp = new ArrayList<Integer>();
    for (int i = 1; i <= n; i++) {
      temp.add(i);
    }
    result.add(temp);
    return result;
  //if k==1
  } else if (k == 1) {

    for (int i = 1; i <= n; i++) {
      ArrayList<Integer> temp = new ArrayList<Integer>();
      temp.add(i);
      result.add(temp);
    }

    return result;
  }

  //for normal cases, initialize a list with one element
  for (int i = 1; i <= n - k + 1; i++) {
    ArrayList<Integer> temp = new ArrayList<Integer>();
    temp.add(i);
    result.add(temp);
  }

  //recursively add more elements
  combine(n, k, result);

  return result;
}

public void combine(int n, int k, ArrayList<ArrayList<Integer>> result) {
  ArrayList<ArrayList<Integer>> prevResult = new
      ArrayList<ArrayList<Integer>>();
  prevResult.addAll(result);

  if(result.get(0).size() == k) return;

  result.clear();
  for (ArrayList<Integer> one : prevResult) {
```

```java
    for (int i = 1; i <= n; i++) {
      if (i > one.get(one.size() - 1)) {
        ArrayList<Integer> temp = new ArrayList<Integer>();
        temp.addAll(one);
        temp.add(i);
        result.add(temp);
      }
    }
  }

  combine(n, k, result);
}
```

147.3 Java Solution 2 - DFS

```java
public ArrayList<ArrayList<Integer>> combine(int n, int k) {
  ArrayList<ArrayList<Integer>> result = new ArrayList<ArrayList<Integer>>();

  if (n <= 0 || n < k)
    return result;

  ArrayList<Integer> item = new ArrayList<Integer>();
  dfs(n, k, 1, item, result); // because it need to begin from 1

  return result;
}

private void dfs(int n, int k, int start, ArrayList<Integer> item,
    ArrayList<ArrayList<Integer>> res) {
  if (item.size() == k) {
    res.add(new ArrayList<Integer>(item));
    return;
  }

  for (int i = start; i <= n; i++) {
    item.add(i);
    dfs(n, k, i + 1, item, res);
    item.remove(item.size() - 1);
  }
}
```

148 Letter Combinations of a Phone Number

Given a digit string, return all possible letter combinations that the number could represent. (Check out your cellphone to see the mappings) Input:Digit string "23", Output: ["ad", "ae", "af", "bd", "be", "bf", "cd", "ce", "cf"].

148.1 Analysis

This problem can be solves by a typical DFS algorithm. DFS problems are very similar and can be solved by using a simple recursion. Check out the index page to see other DFS problems.

148.2 Java Solution

```java
public List<String> letterCombinations(String digits) {
    HashMap<Integer, String> map = new HashMap<Integer, String>();
    map.put(2, "abc");
    map.put(3, "def");
    map.put(4, "ghi");
    map.put(5, "jkl");
    map.put(6, "mno");
    map.put(7, "pqrs");
    map.put(8, "tuv");
    map.put(9, "wxyz");
    map.put(0, "");

    ArrayList<String> result = new ArrayList<String>();

    if(digits == null || digits.length() == 0)
        return result;

    ArrayList<Character> temp = new ArrayList<Character>();
    getString(digits, temp, result, map);

    return result;
}

public void getString(String digits, ArrayList<Character> temp,
    ArrayList<String> result, HashMap<Integer, String> map){
    if(digits.length() == 0){
        char[] arr = new char[temp.size()];
        for(int i=0; i<temp.size(); i++){
            arr[i] = temp.get(i);
        }
        result.add(String.valueOf(arr));
```

```
        return;
    }

    Integer curr = Integer.valueOf(digits.substring(0,1));
    String letters = map.get(curr);
    for(int i=0; i<letters.length(); i++){
       temp.add(letters.charAt(i));
       getString(digits.substring(1), temp, result, map);
       temp.remove(temp.size()-1);
    }
}
```

149 Reverse Integer

LeetCode - Reverse Integer:
Reverse digits of an integer. Example1: x = 123, return 321 Example2: x = -123, return -321

149.1 Naive Method

We can convert the integer to a string/char array, reverse the order, and convert the string/char array back to an integer. However, this will require extra space for the string. It doesn't seem to be the right way, if you come with such a solution.

149.2 Efficient Approach

Actually, this can be done by using the following code.

```
public int reverse(int x) {
  //flag marks if x is negative
  boolean flag = false;
  if (x < 0) {
    x = 0 - x;
    flag = true;
  }

  int res = 0;
  int p = x;

  while (p > 0) {
    int mod = p % 10;
    p = p / 10;
```

```
      res = res * 10 + mod;
   }

   if (flag) {
      res = 0 - res;
   }

   return res;
}
```

149.3 Succinct Solution

This solution is from Sherry, it is succinct and it is pretty.

```
public int reverse(int x) {
   int rev = 0;
   while(x != 0){
      rev = rev*10 + x%10;
      x = x/10;
   }

   return rev;
}
```

149.4 Handle Out of Range Problem

As we form a new integer, it is possible that the number is out of range. We can use the following code to assign the newly formed integer. When it is out of range, throw an exception.

```
try{
  result = ...;
}catch(InputMismatchException exception){
  System.out.println("This is not an integer");
}
```

Please leave your comment if there is any better solutions.

150 Palindrome Number

Determine whether an integer is a palindrome. Do this without extra space.

150.1 Thoughts

Problems related with numbers are frequently solved by / and
   Note: no extra space here means do not convert the integer to string, since string will be a copy of the integer and take extra space. The space take by div, left, and right can be ignored.

150.2 Java Solution

```java
public class Solution {
   public boolean isPalindrome(int x) {
      //negative numbers are not palindrome
      if (x < 0)
        return false;

      // initialize how many zeros
      int div = 1;
      while (x / div >= 10) {
        div *= 10;
      }

      while (x != 0) {
        int left = x / div;
        int right = x % 10;

        if (left != right)
           return false;

        x = (x % div) / 10;
        div /= 100;
      }

      return true;
   }
}
```

151 Pow(x, n)

Problem:
   Implement pow(x, n).
This is a great example to illustrate how to solve a problem during a technical interview. The first and second solution exceeds time limit; the third and fourth are

accepted.

151.1 Naive Method

First of all, assuming n is not negative, to calculate x to the power of n, we can simply multiply x n times, i.e., x * x * ... * x. The time complexity is O(n). The implementation is as simple as:

```
public class Solution {
  public double pow(double x, int n) {
     if(x == 0) return 0;
     if(n == 0) return 1;

     double result=1;
     for(int i=1; i<=n; i++){
        result = result * x;
     }

     return result;
  }
}
```

Now we should think about how to do better than O(n).

151.2 Recursive Method

Naturally, we next may think how to do it in O(logn). We have a relation that $x^n = x^{(n/2)} * x^{(n/2)} * x^{(n$

```
public static double pow(double x, int n) {
  if(n == 0)
     return 1;

  if(n == 1)
     return x;

  int half = n/2;
  int remainder = n%2;


  if(n % 2 ==1 && x < 0 && n < 0)
     return - 1/(pow(-x, half) * pow(-x, half) * pow(-x, remainder));
  else if (n < 0)
     return 1/(pow(x, -half) * pow(x, -half) * pow(x, -remainder));
  else
     return (pow(x, half) * pow(x, half) * pow(x, remainder));
}
```

151 Pow(x, n)

In this solution, we can handle cases that x <0 and n <0. This solution actually takes more time than the first solution. Why?

151.3 Accepted Solution

The accepted solution is also recursive, but does division first. Time complexity is O(nlog(n)). The key part of solving this problem is the while loop.

```
public double pow(double x, int n) {
  if (n == 0)
     return 1;
  if (n == 1)
     return x;

  int pn = n > 0 ? n : -n;// positive n
  int pn2 = pn;

  double px = x > 0 ? x : -x;// positive x
  double result = px;

  int k = 1;
  //the key part of solving this problem
  while (pn / 2 > 0) {
     result = result * result;
     pn = pn / 2;
     k = k * 2;
  }

  result = result * pow(px, pn2 - k);

  // handle negative result
  if (x < 0 && n % 2 == 1)
     result = -result;

  // handle negative power
  if (n < 0)
     result = 1 / result;

  return result;
}
```

151.4 Best Solution

The most understandable solution I have found so far.

```
public double power(double x, int n) {
  if (n == 0)
```

```
    return 1;

  double v = power(x, n / 2);

  if (n % 2 == 0) {
    return v * v;
  } else {
    return v * v * x;
  }
}

public double pow(double x, int n) {
  if (n < 0) {
    return 1 / power(x, -n);
  } else {
    return power(x, n);
  }
}
```

Made in the USA
Las Vegas, NV
04 November 2023